28/9

THE
SHAAR
PRESS

THE JUDAICA IMPRINT
FOR THOUGHTFUL PEOPLE

A SHAAR PRESS PUBLICATION

RABBI ABRAHAM J. TWERSKI, M.D.

The First Year of

MARRIAGE

Enhancing the success of your marriage
right from the start — and even before it begins

Published by **SHAAR PRESS**
Distributed by MESORAH PUBLICATIONS, LTD.
4401 Second Avenue / Brooklyn, N.Y 11232 / (718) 921-9000 / www.artscroll.com

Distributed in Israel by SIFRIATI / A. GITLER
6 Hayarkon Street / Bnei Brak 51127

Distributed in Europe by LEHMANNS
Unit E, Viking Business Park, Rolling Mill Road / Jarrow, Tyne and Wear, NE32 3DP/ England

Distributed in Australia and New Zealand by GOLDS WORLD OF JUDAICA
3-13 William Street / Balaclava, Melbourne 3183 / Victoria Australia

Distributed in South Africa by KOLLEL BOOKSHOP
Shop 8A Norwood Hypermarket / Norwood 2196, Johannesburg, South Africa

ISBN: 1-57819-432-6 Hard Cover
ISBN: 1-57819-433-4 Paperback

Printed in the United States of America by Noble Book Press
Custom bound by Sefercraft, Inc. / 4401 Second Avenue / Brooklyn N.Y. 11232

Acknowledgments

*I wish to express my sincere gratitude to my wife,
Dr. Gail Bessler Twerski, for her invaluable insights
and comments, and to Judi Dick for her superb
editing. I am also grateful to several people who
took the time and effort to review the book and
make constructive comments. (I was especially
pleased with the comment, "Where were you
twenty-five years ago when I needed you?")*

Table of Contents

Introduction

*T*here is a startling statement in the Talmud: "R' Eliezer says: An *adam* (person) who does not have a wife is not an *adam*, because the Torah says, 'He created them male and female—and called them *adam*' "(*Genesis* 5:2). One has an identity as a *whole* person only when one is married.

The Torah relates how Eve was created from part of Adam. Rashi cites the Midrash which states that Adam and Eve were created fused together, and what is described as the creation of Eve is that they were separated (ibid. 1:27). Yes, separated, but joined again as a unit by marriage.

There is no question that the secret of Jewish survival through centuries of exile and persecution is the strength and stability of the family.* Nothing is as dear in Judaism as *shalom bayis*, a peaceful

---

* The Talmud states that the *Beis HaMikdash* is not as Abraham said, a mountain, and not as Yitzchak said, a field, but as Jacob said, a house (*Pesachim* 88a). One of the commentaries extends this concept to the survival of the Jewish nation. Some say it is the ability of Jews to overcome major obstacles. Others say it is the courage and bravery of Jews to win on the battlefield. But it is neither of these, not the "mountain" of

and harmonious home. "One who instills peace within the home is considered as though he instilled peace throughout the Jewish nation" (*Avos D'Rebbi Nosson* 28). The final *berachah* at the *chuppah* states that G-d created for the young couple: "joy and gladness; mirth, glad song, pleasure, delight, love, brotherhood, peace and companionship." In the most difficult of times, this ideal of Jewish marriage was pursued. It is within reach.

Today, something is obviously wrong.

The incidence of divorce in the United States among couples who marry before age 24 is 30 percent (U.S. Census Bureau, cited in *Newsweek*, 3/1/04). Thus, in the general population, one out of three marriages in this age group fails. There are no accurate statistics for the divorce rate among Jews, but even if it is a third of that, it is still an intolerable incidence. Not only are the partners affected, but the effects on any offspring will inevitably be damaging.

Traditionally, divorce among Torah-observant Jews was rather rare. Granted, some couples may have continued in an unhappy marriage because of the social disapproval of divorce, but that, too, is fading. Divorce among Torah-observant couples today is anything but a rarity.

Changes in the prevailing culture have undoubtedly influenced the relationship between Torah-observant couples. However, marriage counselors have confirmed my observation that young people are woefully unprepared for marriage. Their misconceptions give rise to conflicts, which seem to be self-reinforcing. By the time they seek competent counseling (if they do), much serious damage to the relationship may already have occurred.

Unfortunately, in many families, more time is spent on the arrangements for the wedding, which will last only several hours, than for the couple's relationship, which should last a lifetime.

Just as young people are inadequately prepared for their new roles as husbands and wives, their parents may be equally unpre-

---

Abraham nor the "field" of Yitzchak, but rather the "house" of Jacob. It is the sanctity of the Jewish home that is our survival.

Our beginning as a nation was with the Exodus from Egypt. How was a people who were essentially dehumanized by decades of torture to become a nation? The first mitzvah given to the Jewish people on the eve of the Exodus was the *korban pesach*, "They shall take for themselves a lamb for each father's house...for the *household*" (*Exodus* 12:3). A *family* mitzvah was the basis of our nationhood.

pared for their roles as parents-in-law. Sometimes unrealistic demands of the young couple are made, and what may be intended as helpful advice may be perceived as meddling and as an invasion of their privacy.

Understandably, much of the difficulty occurs at the beginning of the marriage. If problems can be averted or dealt with in the first year, the likelihood of a smooth marriage relationship is greatly increased. The Torah recognizes the importance of the first year of marriage, providing the husband an exemption not only from military duty, but also from all community obligations. The newlywed must be freed from stress in order that he should "gladden his wife" (*Deuteronomy* 24:5).

A better understanding of the more common sources of misunderstanding and potential conflict during the early phase of marriage may prevent much distress. The purpose of this book is to facilitate the process of adjustment so that the ideal of "a single unit" can be achieved.

What I am proposing in this book are concepts that I believe can prevent some of the misunderstandings. These are not inviolable rules. Rather, they are points for consideration by both partners to the marriage, which should facilitate a harmonious relationship.

It Is Not "Business as Usual"

*H*uman beings are creatures of habit. We develop behavior patterns that become our second nature. Altering any way of feeling or acting, behavior that has been ingrained for years, frequently meets with resistance.

The Talmud says that just as people are dissimilar in their facial features, they are also dissimilar in their ideation. It is axiomatic that there are differences in the way people think, and this is also true of a husband and wife. Some differences are minor, others more significant, but regardless of their magnitude, these differences may result in disagreement. Adjustment to each other's ideation is essential for a harmonious marriage.

I often wonder when I see people kiss the *mezuzah* whether this is just a perfunctory gesture, or do they really get the message of the *mezuzah*. People who do think about the *mezuzah* generally think of it as an assertion of the unity of G-d (*Shema Yisrael*), which it certainly is. However, there is an additional important message that may be overlooked.

The *mezuzah* is affixed to the door in a diagonal position. This is so because there are two opinions in halachah. One is that the *mezuzah* should be vertical, and the other is that it should be horizontal. The diagonal position is, therefore, a *compromise* between the two.

Each time you kiss the *mezuzah*, you should remember the wisdom and importance of compromise. The parchment of the *mezuzah* protects the home, and the message of compromise delivered by its diagonal position serves to protect the marriage.

Having said that, I wish to make a caveat, and I beg of you not to distort it. As commendable as compromise is, there may be a situation where each partner wishes to hold onto his/her opinion. Couples can be happy even if they do not agree on some things, *as long as they respect the other's opinion* and as long as their divergent opinions do not result in any dysfunction.*

Young people may have fantasies that their relationship will be so idyllic that there will never be any need for adjustments. "I know that everything will be okay. I'll gladly do whatever he/she wants to keep him/her happy." The reality is, however, that some adjustments are invariably necessary.

The very first thing newlyweds should know is that *they must undergo some change*, and that changing a pattern of behavior may be difficult. It is also very important to know that *the only person you can change is yourself.* You cannot change another person. Hopefully, when you make changes in yourself, your partner will **likewise** make some changes.

Marriage brings about a totally new role, different from anything young people have ever experienced. One is no longer an individual and one is no longer a child relating to parents. One is now a

---

*At chassidic weddings, it is customary to have a "Rebbe Reb Melech Dance." This dance is said to have originated with the chassidic master R' Elimelech of Lizhensk. People pair up, and several pairs dance toward each other. When they meet, one pair raises their arms to form an arch, and the others bow down, dancing under the arch. On meeting the next pair, the pair that bowed and danced under the arch now raise their arms to form an arch, and the oncoming pair bows and goes under their arch. With multiple pairs, the dance is very graceful.

If one pair fails to raise their arms at the proper time or a pair fails to bow when it is their turn, the two pairs collide. The message is that in order to avoid collision, sometimes you are the one who yields, and sometimes it is the other partner who yields.

husband or wife. Ways of acting that were previously appropriate may now be inappropriate.

The point I wish to make here has some application even in the first year of marriage, but becomes of increasing importance as the family grows.

A family is a *system*, comprised of *interacting parts.* It is helpful to think of the family as a "mobile," i.e., the configuration of little animal figures suspended over an infant's crib. When it is left alone, it is stable, in equilibrium, with each little animal being in a particular place. If you move any one animal ever so slightly, all the other little animals change their positions, arriving at a new equilibrium. It is impossible to move any animal without causing a corresponding readjustment in the positions of all the other little animals.

A family is a *system in equilibrium.* Like the mobile, the family is always at an equilibrium. *Any change in any one member of the family inevitably results in a change of some type in every other member.* It cannot be otherwise.

In a newlywed couple, the nuclear family has only two parts. (Of course, the extended family, too, is a system which follows the principle of the mobile.) Husband and wife should know that any change in either of them will perforce result in some adjustment of the other. As new members join the family, the system becomes more complex, and any change in any single member of the family will result in a corresponding change in *all* family members.

The passion of an early love relationship may distort one's perception and judgment. In the intensity of emotion, the young man and young woman may see themselves as perfectly compatible. Any differences are either completely denied or are thought to be insignificant. Indeed, a noted authority on couples counseling, Dr. Harley Hendrix, says that marriages that are arranged by match rather than by "falling in love" have a better chance of survival. The couple is paired according to the evaluation of their compatibility by people with more objective judgment, who have not been blinded by emotion to differences that may be very substantial.*

---

*The European social critic Denis de Rougemont (quoted in *The Second Time Around,* Janda & MacCormack, Carol Publications, p. 21) stated: "The notion of marrying for love is one of the most pathological experiments that a civilized society has ever imagined, the basing of a marriage, which is lasting, upon romance, which is a passing fancy."

In earlier days, it was customary that the bride and groom would not meet before the wedding. I must admit that I have some difficulty advocating this, although I did observe a beautiful marriage between my parents. My father first met my mother *after* the *chuppah*. In the secular culture, people marry someone they love. Perhaps it is more important to love someone you marry than to marry someone you love.

Young people have fantasies about marriage. Whether or not they have been exposed to fairy tales that end with, "and they lived happily ever after," they may think that marriage will eliminate all their problems. The spouse will shower them with love and tend to all their needs. They will not only be loved, but also respected and highly valued by the partner. Even boys and girls whose parents' marriage was turbulent may think, "I will never be like my father/mother," or "he/she will never be like my father/mother. We will have a great marriage."

Marriage can be fulfilling, and it is indeed possible for couples to find in each other what they had been lacking. However, anticipation that marriage will make "everything bad in my life disappear" is unrealistic and may result in disillusionment.

Parents of children who have emotional or psychological difficulties may similarly believe, "Once he/she is married, he/she will settle down." Parents need to be made aware that marriage is not a hospital and does not cure anything. To the contrary, problems that existed in an individual prior to marriage are likely to be accentuated after marriage.

It is true that marriage can help make a person whole. The *Zohar* refers to an unmarried person as "half a body" (*Zohar* 3:81). A person is whole only in marriage. But this refers to a marriage where there is an emotional fusion of two people. The mere contractual relationship of marriage does not result in wholeness.

Problems may surface even early in the honeymoon. One young woman, leaving her parents' home after the week of *sheva berachos*, was tearful. "Everything I ever was, I am leaving behind me. I'm not even taking my own name along." The anxiety of dispensing with a familiar relationship and an identity of long-standing to assume a new role and identity may result in feelings of insecurity. Venturing into the unknown may be frightening even when the expectations are pleasant. These fears may be calmed only by a great deal of reassurance, which is not always forthcoming in newlyweds, especially since both partners may be experiencing similar anxiety.

It seems immaterial whether the couple met frequently during the engagement, met infrequently, had only phone contact or no contact at all. Whichever, many points of potential disagreement are generally not discussed. For example, in the young man's family, it was not unusual to leave the supper dishes in the sink to be done the next morning. The young woman's mother would have suffered a heart attack if the kitchen were not spotless before she retired. I have seen serious arguments arise when there are significant differences in the couple's concepts of orderliness and cleanliness. She may consider the husband's laxity as slovenly and disgusting, and he may see the wife's perfectionism as intolerable compulsivity. But who even thinks of discussing issues such as this prior to marriage? Both partners may be in for an unpleasant surprise. For such a marriage to be smooth, some change must occur, preferably in both partners.

Or, the young man's father was not too punctilious about special occasions such as birthdays and anniversaries. Sometimes he remembered, sometimes he did not. It was never a big thing in his family. The young woman's father never missed celebrating such occasions, often with fanfare. To overlook a birthday or an anniversary was catastrophic. The first time the newlywed husband does not remember an auspicious occasion, he may find his wife in tears, accusing him of not caring about her feelings or indeed, about her.

Or, the young man's father and mother always chose furniture and drapes together. Both had their input in the interior decoration. The young woman's father left all such decisions to his wife, and was pleased with whatever she chose. Assuming that all husbands are alike, the newlywed wife furnishes the house without consulting the husband, who may become upset because she does not consider his wishes and opinions as important.

Or, a rather common occurrence. The young man's father made the bank deposits, decided which bills to pay and wrote out the checks. His mother would ask permission before making significant purchases. The young man assumes that this is indeed the husband's role. The young woman's parents managed all finances together.

She wants to have input in writing checks and making financial decisions. To her, the husband's desire to be the sole manager of finances constitutes control. The husband does not see this as a control issue at all, but simply as the proper role of a husband.

Or, while the husband is at work or in school, the wife goes shopping with her mother and they spend the afternoon together. She did not call her husband to tell him about this, because she did not think it was necessary. She does not carry a cell-phone. The husband calls home at lunch and numerous times after that, and when there is no answer, he panics. When he comes home he is inordinately angry at her for having caused him so much anxiety that he could not get anything done at the office or at school.

Or, the wife is very close to her family, and wants to spend every Friday night meal with them, just as her sister and her brother-in-law do. The husband, on the other hand, would like a quiet Friday night at home, just the two of them alone. The wife may feel that he is inconsiderate of her feelings and that if he really loved her, he would agree to Friday nights at her parents' home.

The possibilities of areas of disagreement are legion, and it is virtually impossible to discuss all details of married life prior to marriage. What each partner should know is that the other partner may have ideas that are substantially different, and that change will be necessary. For one partner to assume a fixed position and insist that the other partner must change to accommodate is unreasonable, and can lead to the dire consequences of a power struggle or a master-slave relationship. Neither of these is conducive to a happy marriage.

Each partner has a lifestyle with which he/she feels comfortable, but, as a rule, the partners do not formulate the components of their lifestyle in so many words to themselves, let alone verbalize them to each other. If each partner could think about his/her own lifestyle, try to put it into words and exchange these ideas with the other partner, they could discuss them, come to an agreement and avoid painful altercations.

Dr. Les Parrott says, "Two independent persons forming a way of life together eventually run into power struggles and must learn to adjust to each other's ways. The intensity and turmoil of this stage vary among couples, but almost every couple engages in the struggle. Successful passage through this stage enables each partner to say, 'Okay. So I am willing to admit that my romance with a perfect partner is an illusion. However, I am still fascinated with the mystery of who you are, and I am willing to pursue romance with you and journey together toward a more mature love' " (*Saving Your Marriage Before It Starts*, p. 42).

It is safe to assume that the young husband and wife may have different ways of doing some things, but they can discover these differences only *after* they are married. People tend to think that the way they do something is *the* right way. When differences are discovered, each partner should respect the other partner's way, and then come to an understanding of how they would like things in their marriage.

We often hear it said that marriage is a 50/50 proposition. That is not necessarily true. Sometimes it may be 50/50, and at other times it may be 75/25, and sometimes it may be 100/0. With mutual respect and consideration, even major differences can be worked out to a mutually satisfactory accommodation.

The following is an example of a rather minor difference.

The wife returns from Friday shopping to discover that the husband is putting up the *cholent*. "What are you doing?" she asks.

"I'm putting up the *cholent*," he says.

"But that's my job," she says.

"My father always puts up the *cholent*," the husband responds. "He says that this is his part in *kevod Shabbos*. Didn't you like the *cholent* at our house."

The wife laughs. "Sure, it was great. My father doesn't know anything in the kitchen. Do you really like putting up the *cholent*?"

"Sure," the husband says, "unless you prefer to do it."

"Okay," the wife says, "let's see how it turns out. Next week I'll do it, and we'll decide which one we like better."

This sounds rather trivial, but there is a story of how a minor difference brought a couple to a Rebbe for a settlement of their dispute.

A couple consulted the Rebbe of Koznitz, because they had a difference in a *minhag*. In the husband's home, the *kugel* was served with the Shabbos morning *Kiddush*. In the wife's home, the *kugel* was served during the meal. Each spouse wanted to preserve the respective family *minhag*.

The Rebbe suggested that they have *two* kugels, one at *Kiddush* and the other during the meal.

There can be differences that are more weighty than *cholent* and *kugel*, but the point is that differences can be worked out. As long as each partner respects the other's position, satisfactory solutions can be found.

In the wife's family, Friday night was a time for socializing, getting together at someone's home after the Friday night meal to shmooze and partake of refreshments. The husband would rather have a quiet Friday night. At the end of a workweek, socializing is not his thing. "Okay, let's try alternating. One Friday night with friends, the next at home alone. Let's see how that works out." Each one yields a bit.

How a couple accommodates on a particular point is not all-important. What is important is that they discuss instead of having a "knee-jerk" reaction. They may come to a conclusion other than "splitting down the middle," but whatever they decide, it is not likely to end up in a heated argument about who is right.

I heard a man say, "My wife and I used to fight a great deal. Of course, I did not want to lose a fight. But I realized that if I won, that meant she lost. I did not want to be married to a loser, so we stopped fighting and began discussing instead.

Or there may be this scenario:

WIFE: I'd like to eat out once a week. I'm glad to cook dinner after I get home from work, but I'd like one night a week off.

HUSBAND: I don't object in principle, but it's difficult on a tight budget. How about if I relieve you and cook dinner one night a week?

WIFE: Hey, if you can cook, we ought to split the kitchen duties. You can cook dinner three nights a week.

HUSBAND: Maybe we can fit eating out once a week into the budget after all.

How about this one:

HUSBAND: I don't like credit cards. If you have to pay cash, you think a bit more whether or not to buy the thing.

	With credit cards you don't think about the bill that's going to come, plus the 18 percent interest.
WIFE:	I can agree to that. I can take out checks from the checkbook before I go shopping.
HUSBAND:	No, that's not good. Sometimes you forget to fill in the stub when you come back, or you forget the exact amount, and that messes up the checkbook.
WIFE:	Okay, How about if I have a separate account and carry a small checkbook in my purse?

Again, the couple may decide on other options. This is totally different than the husband opening up the credit card bill and screaming, "For heavens sake! Why did you have to buy that picture? Look at the amount we owe. If we don't pay it all off, we are hit with 18 percent interest next month."

There are several sources of potential conflict in a relationship. Each partner may naively assume that the other partner has similar ideas, or that if there are any dissimilarities, they are of little consequence and fade into nothingness in the basking of their love. Or, if there are any significant differences, "he/she will change."

It has been suggested that women are attracted to men who have similarities to their father, and that men are attracted to women who have similarities to their mother. I don't know whether this is true or how often these similarities influence their choices. Some of these factors may be operative in the subconscious, so that although the woman protests that she will never marry a man who is even remotely like her father, her subconscious directs her precisely in that direction.

I recall a woman who complained bitterly about her husband's drinking and related how her mother had suffered the grief of an alcoholic marriage. I asked, "Did you have any idea before you were married that Tim drank more than he should?" The woman answered affirmatively. "Then why," I asked, "if you saw your mother's suffering, did you marry a man who you knew drank too much?" Her answer was, "I thought he would change for me." This in spite of her observing that her mother's efforts to get her father to change were absolutely futile.

In those instances where a woman divorces an alcoholic husband, the odds are that she will marry another alcoholic. Where is the logic in this? There may be none, but the facts speak for themselves.

One woman, whose father was emotionally abusive to her mother, sought help because her husband was verbally abusive to her. There had been clear signs of inconsideration and controlling behavior in her *chassan*. They had met only a few times during their engagement, and on these occasions, as well as in their phone conversations, he teased and belittled her. Rather than consider this a warning sign, she thought it was "cute."

The false assumption, "I can change him/her," is the source of much misery. Keep this in mind: "What you see is what you get." Of course, people can change, but only when *they* want to change. *You* cannot make a person change. You can change how you respond, and if you change your response, your spouse may decide to make a change, too.

My dear newlyweds: you are to be each other's *partner* in life, not a father, mother, teacher or therapist, just a husband/wife, and that should be the only relationship between you.

Unless there is significant pathology in either spouse, sensible people can make an accommodation and adjust to each other's differences. This may take some patience and work by both partners, who need to work to understand each other.

"Understand." That is a key word. Let's take it literally, to "stand-under." If you were able to stand under a person, experience what he/she experiences, sees and feels, then you could really *understand* the person.

One of the side-effects of modern life has been that patience and willingness to work things out are often in short supply. Technology has eroded our tolerance for endurance. Jet planes, fax machines, instant foods and microwave ovens have habituated us to want and to expect results immediately. Willingness to repair relationships has suffered from the "disposable age." In my youth, a fountain pen was a valued object. The Sheaffer pen I received for my Bar Mitzvah was a treasured companion for twenty years, and I felt an attachment to it. Today's cheap ballpoint pens are "throw-aways." No one would bother to have a radio or tape recorder repaired. (You probably could not even find anyone who does such repairs.) If it malfunctions, dispose of it and get a new one. The list of disposables includes diapers, tableware, contact lenses and even cameras and pots (yes, pots!).

The lack of meaningful attachments to objects, which would warrant repairing and keeping them, has had an influence on human relationships as well. The alarming incidence of divorce may be due in no small part to an attitude of, "Don't bother trying to fix a relationship. Just discard it and get a new one."

But people are not objects, and should not be treated as such. If we treat other people as objects, we become objects ourselves and lose our dignity as "created in the likeness of G-d." While there are relationships that are in fact incompatible, many could be salvaged. The best way to do so is to establish the relationship on a sound foundation.

That's what this book is about.

Romance Versus True Love

*A*lthough abiding by the dictum, "What you see is what you get," would seem to avoid disillusionment, it is not a foolproof guide. The reason: one may not see correctly.

Just as it is generally true that "we believe what we want to believe," it is also true that "we see what we want to see." I have seen instances where the warning signs were as prominent as flashing lights, but were ignored. This was not so much because one anticipated change, but because one was simply oblivious of the nature of the other person's character.

The Torah states a crucial principle: "You shall not accept a bribe, for the bribe *will blind the eyes of the wise*" (*Deuteronomy* 16:19). The meaning, of course, is that a bribe will distort the judge's critical faculty to favor the litigant who bribed him. But I suggest that we take the verse more literally rather than as a metaphor. A judge who has been bribed *cannot see* facts that favor the opposing litigant or that are unfavorable to the briber. He has been *blinded*, and just as one cannot get a blind person to see, regardless of how logical and convincing one may be, neither can a judge who has accepted a bribe see the facts as they are.

This is true of every human being. We can all have psychological blindness. When the Talmud says that "A person does not see his own defects" (*Shabbos* 119a), it means just that. Pointing them out to him may be as futile as pointing out a painting to a blind person. Psychological blindness is as real as physical blindness.

A young woman may have an idealized image of her *chassan*, and he may have an idealized image of his *kallah*. They see each other this way because they want to. This desire may blind them to all character blemishes. They are bribed by this fantasy and are rendered psychologically blind by this bribe.

The romance and passion at the beginning of a relationship are a beautiful blossom. Just as the blossom falls off and is replaced by the fruit, so the honeymoon of the romance fades away and should be replaced by true, mature love.

When the romance phase passes, whether in three months or two years, the blinders are removed, and each person may now see in the other something of which they were unaware. Unless they are prepared for this, the discovery of traits which are displeasing can come as a shock and result in disillusionment. The knowledge that the other person is a human being and may have some character defects may prevent the disappointment of disillusionment.

Let us remember that character defects are what make us human. It would be most uncomfortable to live with someone who is a celestial angel. It has been wisely said, "G-d help the man who won't marry until he finds a perfect woman, and G-d help him still more if he finds her." This does not mean that one should overlook character defects, but rather that one should not be surprised to discover them.

A person may feel that he/she is absolutely honest and is revealing everything about oneself, but because a person may be unaware of one's character defects, one cannot reveal something one does not know.

Yitzchak did not tell Eidel that he was a narcissist because he did not think he was. (A narcissist is someone who is totally absorbed with himself, expects everybody to adore him, thinks the world owes him a living and never thinks himself to be at fault.) The information Eidel's parents had was that he was of fine character. No one in the yeshivah was aware of his narcissism, or if they were, they did not report it. Shortly after their wedding Eidel realized that there was a problem. Yitzchak expected to be waited on hand-and-foot. If Eidel said anything that he took as criticism he would flare up.

Unfortunately, Eidel had no way of knowing that Yitzchak was a narcissist. Seeing that there was a problem, Eidel suggested that they see a marriage counselor, which Yitzchak refused, because he felt there was nothing wrong with him. Narcissism is a stubborn character defect, and if it is discovered, the spouse should avail himself/herself of competent counseling.

What is true love? This is defined by the Talmud: "to love a wife as much as he loves himself" (*Yevamos* 62b). We will elaborate on this a bit later.

Although we may enjoy the beauty of a blossom, we know that it must fall away in order for the fruit to emerge. Similarly, the fading of the romance and fantasy of the early relationship should not be seen as a loss. It allows the relationship to develop into a much deeper and more meaningful intimacy.

In the introduction, I cited the last of the seven *berachos* of the marriage ceremony, that G-d created the *chassan* and *kallah*, along with "joy and gladness; mirth, glad song, pleasure, delight, love, brotherhood, peace and companionship." Whereas the joy and gladness; mirth and glad song are most conspicuous at the wedding celebration, pleasure, delight, love, brotherhood, peace and companionship should prevail throughout married life. These are features that G-d created. They exist and are accessible. If we do not have them, it is because we are derelict in acquiring them.

"Pleasure and delight." Yes, one can experience pleasure and delight with a tasty dish of food, a new garment or a new car. While there is no reason to deprive ourselves of these, they are not the kind of pleasure and delight that G-d intended to characterize marriage.

The gustatory pleasure of a gourmet dish exists only as long as one is eating, and at the very most, a few moments afterward. Strangely enough, an attractive dress may appear charming on the rack in the store, but how long before it is demoted to the status of "the *shmattes* (rags) in the closet"? The thrill of a new car seldom persists beyond the presence of the "new car smell." Transient feelings such as these do not give a marriage "staying power."

But think of the feelings you have from having done a kindness to someone. This pleasant sensation can be with you for years. In fact, nothing can eradicate or even diminish it. Commenting on the verse, "what a man gives to the Kohen shall be his" (*Numbers* 5:10), one of the expositors on Torah relates that when Baron Rothschild was asked how much he owns, he responded, "That which I gave to *tzedakah* is all that I can really say I own. All my other possessions may be lost."

In an inspiring essay, R' Eliyahu Dessler says that the popular conception that one gives to whomever one loves is fallacious. Rather, he says, *one loves to whomever one gives* (*Michtav MeEliyahu*, vol. 1 p. 32). Giving to another person generates love. When you give of yourself to another person, you invest something of yourself in him. Inasmuch as "a person is closest to himself" (*Sanhedrin* 9b), you are automatically drawn toward that part of yourself that is now within him.

When the emphasis is "What can I *give* to this relationship?" rather than "What can I *get* from this relationship?" there can be true love.

The chassidic master, R' Moshe Leib of Sassov, said that he learned what true love is by overhearing a dialogue between two inebriates.

"Stephan," the first man said, "I love you with all my heart."

"No, Ivan," Stephan said. "You do not love me." Ivan, in his drunkenness, began crying. "I swear, Stephan, I love you with all my heart."

Stephan responded, "If you truly love me, Ivan, then tell me, what do I need and where do I hurt."

R' Moshe Leib said, "If you do not feel another person's needs and his pain, you do not love him."

True love goes beyond passion, and is comprised of brotherhood, friendship and commitment. Brotherhood and friendship are the constituents of intimacy, without which a marriage is nothing but two people living under the same roof. Intimacy means mutual honesty, trust, sharing, support and closeness. It provides the feeling that one is accepted for what one is.

What is commitment? Try this definition: The difference between interest and commitment is that when you are interested in something, you do it only when it is convenient. When you are committed to something, you make no excuses, and give it everything you've got. Committed people desire the successful outcome of their pursuits with astounding intensity. There is no room for apathy or lessened motivation. Commitment provides a constant source of renewal and energy.

It is not enough to *feel* love for another. It must be manifested in a way that is appreciated and absorbed by the other; i.e., by *giving* of yourself to another.

The Talmud relates an incident of a couple who were childless ten years after their marriage. Inasmuch as each desired progeny, they came to R' Shimon bar Yochai for a divorce. R' Shimon said, "This is not a divorce because of mutual dislike. Therefore, just as there was a festive celebration at your marriage, there must be a festive celebration at the divorce."

The couple followed R' Shimon's advice, and made a lavish party. The husband said to his wife, "My dear, you should return to your father's home. Take with you whatever it is that you cherish most."

Having eaten and imbibed heavily, the husband fell asleep. The wife then had her servants carry him to her father's home. When he awoke, he said to his wife, "Where am I?" The wife said, "You are in my father's home." "What am I doing here?" the husband asked. The wife said, "Didn't you tell me I should take whatever I cherished most to my father's home? It is you that I love more than anything in the world."

They returned to R' Shimon, who prayed for them, and they were blessed with children (*Midrash Rabbah, Shir HaShirim* 1:30).

Obviously, this couple had much love for each other. However, it took a decisive act of manifesting this love to override all other considerations.

As I pointed out earlier, low self-esteem is very prevalent. It is a safe assumption that one's spouse has at least some element of low self-esteem, although it may not be readily apparent. People with low self-esteem are often fearful of being rejected, and mutual commitment in marriage is very reassuring.

Commitment means looking forward to a future together, sharing dreams, enjoying their fulfillment together and tolerating their frustrations together. In many marriages, there may be "rough spots," and in the "disposable era," in which we have become accustomed to throwing away things that we do not feel are functioning optimally rather than making the effort to repair them, *commitment* is a vital ingredient in marriage.

True love in a marriage must be attained and maintained. Even true love can wither if not nurtured. It is much like losing weight. A person may go on a "crash diet" and lose weight, but unless a reasonable diet is maintained over the long term, the weight is soon regained. The components of true love must be continuously practiced if the love is to endure.

I am told that a jetliner uses a great deal of its fuel in the takeoff. But as crucial as the takeoff is, it does not get you to your destination. Major adjustments may indeed have to be made in the beginning of marriage, but they need to continue, if only at a less intense level.

Feelings are not etched in stone, and they may fluctuate. There are so many variables in a marriage, both internal and external, that the same degree of feeling may vary from day to day. The advent of children, the change of a career, illness, children growing up and leaving home, economic stresses and grief are just some of the things that may affect how a person feels. Changes in feelings should be expected and should not be misinterpreted as indicating instability of the marriage.

A Firm Foundation

*O*ur sages have provided us with the ingredients to begin marriage with a firm foundation. Unfortunately, too often we do not pay adequate attention to their words.

The sages of the Talmud formulated *berachos* which are chanted at the wedding ceremony after the husband seals the marriage contract with giving the ring and reciting: *"Harei at mekudeshes li,* You are hereby sanctified to me." The first *berachah* states: *shehakol bara lichvodo,* that G-d created everything for His glory. The second *berachah* states: *yotzer haadam,* that G-d created man. We are familiar with these *berachos,* but how often have we given much thought to their relevance in the wedding ceremony?

Marriage counselors say that problems in a marriage often arise because of difficulties in communication. While this is undoubtedly true, there is another consideration. This insight came to me at the airport.

I was standing on the moving sidewalk, and parallel to it was a moving sidewalk going in the opposite direction. Next to me stood an airline employee, who noticed another airline employee on the adjacent moving sidewalk. They exchanged a few words, but soon could not communicate because they were out of range, heading in opposite directions. It occurred to me that although they may have had excellent communication skills, they could not communicate because they were moving away from one another, each headed in a different direction.

In his book, *Getting the Love You Want*, Dr. Harley Hendrix says, "After all, people don't get married to take care of their partner's needs—they get married to further their own psychological and emotional growth." It should be evident that marriages such as this *are not based on a common interest.* The husband and wife do not have the same goal. The man is interested primarily in having *his* needs met, and the woman is interested primarily in having *her* needs met. Like the two people on the moving sidewalks, they may be going in opposite directions. Even if their communication skills are excellent, they cannot communicate effectively because they are, in fact, distant from each other (unless they shout, which happens only too often). If there is a shortcoming in having their own needs met, the very foundation of the marriage is threatened.

Our sages, therefore, give the young couple inestimable advice: *shehakol bara lichvodo.* Everything must be for the glory of G-d. While there is no denying that each person needs his/her emotional needs satisfied, *that should not be the primary basis for this marriage.* The primary goal of this marriage is *kevod Shamayim*, to establish a family and home that will bring greater glory to G-d. Even if one or both partners may feel that all their emotional needs have not been satisfied, the basis of the relationship is not weakened. As long as the foundation is intact, correcting any shortcomings is much more readily accomplished.

The human being is a composite entity, comprised of a body and a spirit. The body is essentially an animal body. What distinguishes a human being from animals is not the body, but the *spirit.* In *Twerski on Spirituality*, I have defined the human spirit as being comprised of all the traits that are unique to man and are absent in animals.

Man is the only living creature that can learn from the history of past generations—to avoid mistakes they made and build upon their positive accomplishments. Man is the only living thing that can reflect on the purpose of life and contemplate an ultimate goal in life. Man is the only being that can seek to improve himself voluntarily by his own efforts. (Caterpillars do improve when they become butterflies, but this is an automatic process programmed in their genes, and they do not willfully decide to become butterflies.) Man is the only being that can think about the future consequences of his actions. Man is the only being that can delay gratification, and man is the only living thing that can make ethical and moral decisions, in defiance of bodily drives and urges.

All animal behavior is self-centered. With the exception of domesticated pets that may adopt human traits, the nature of an animal is to satisfy all its desires. An animal will not sacrifice its comfort for the benefit of another animal (except for mothers animals, which have a biological feeling for their young). The ability to put another's needs ahead of one's own is uniquely human, and is one of the important distinctions between man and animals.

The desire to have all one's needs met is self-centeredness, hence it is an animal rather than a human trait. To put it bluntly, a marriage that is predicated on having one's own needs met is essentially an animal-type relationship. If the goal is primarily one's own gratification, it stands to reason that if either partner feels that another person could do a better job at providing that gratification, the terms of the contract are void.

But a person is *not* an animal. A person is a *mentsch,* who was created when G-d "blew a breath of life into him." As the *Zohar* says, the Torah uses this metaphor because when one exhales, he exhales something from within himself. Therefore, when G-d "blew a breath of life" into man, He put something of Himself into him. Man, therefore, has a Divine *neshamah,* and it should be beneath one's dignity to ignore the *neshamah* and behave solely based on the body's desire for gratification, which is animalistic behavior. A person must be a *mentsch,* who is able to sacrifice his comfort and personal needs for the benefit of others.

The young couple is, therefore, reminded—*yotzer haadam.* G-d created you as a unique human being, not as an animal. Each of you must be the *mentsch* that you were created to be. You must be able to sacrifice, to set aside your own needs and desires for your partner, assuming, of course, that your partner is a *mentsch*. One need not make sacrifices for a narcissist

The change from being a single, self-centered person to being married and devoted to the needs of one's spouse is *mentschlichkeit*, and as was noted earlier, one is not an *adam*, a *mentsch*, until one is whole, as a husband-and-wife unit, hence *yotzer haadam*.

The third *berachah* states that G-d created woman *from* man. I alluded to this in the introduction. The concept of a fusion into a single unit is conveyed by the story of R' Aryeh Levin (*A Tzaddik In Our Time*, Feldheim Publishers, 1978) whose wife consulted a physician because of a painful foot. It is related that R' Levin said to the doctor, "Our foot hurts."

What kind of unit is marriage? I found a definition that is appropriate. "Marriage resembles a pair of shears, so joined that they cannot be separated, often moving in opposite directions, yet always punishing anyone who comes between them."

The Jerusalem Talmud points out that if a person sustains an injury to his arm, he does not strike the arm for having caused him pain (*Nedarim* 9:4). If the awareness of being a single unit can be achieved, the reaction toward feeling a discomfort caused by the other spouse would not result in retaliatory behavior.

In keeping with the practice of remembering Jerusalem on all joyous occasions, the next *berachah* is a prayer for G-d to bring joy to Jerusalem with the return of her children in the Ultimate Redemption.

The sixth *berachah* is a prayer that G-d gladden the "beloved companions." Inasmuch as at this point, the relationship is just beginning and the couple may not as yet have reached the stage of "beloved," it is on the assumption that love will indeed develop. The reference point is the gladness of Adam and Eve in Gan Eden, who, as is evident in the account of Creation, knew for certain that they were a single unit. The understanding that their new relationship should forge a single unit is the key to their becoming "beloved."

A marriage based on *shehakol bara lichvodo*, to bring greater glory to G-d rather than to oneself, on *yotzer haadam*, on the uniqueness of the ability to make personal sacrifices for the other partner, and on the realization that husband and wife are a single unit can be a happy marriage and of long duration

It is only after these *berachos* that we invoke G-d's blessing to "give happiness to the beloved companions." The principle that "G-d will bless you in all that you do" (*Deuteronomy* 15:18) applies here. We can receive His blessing for happiness only if we adopt the teachings of the earlier *berachos.*

Taking Control
of Your Behavior

*T*here is one extremely important thing that we must know about our behavior.

As rational people, we feel that we know why we do things.

When I leave the house for the office in the morning, I know why I am doing that. When I insert the key and turn on the ignition, I know why I am doing that. If you were to ask me about every move I make at the office, I could give you a logical reason for everything. Perhaps infants may act haphazardly, but mature adults act with knowledge of what they are doing (albeit not always intelligently and responsibly).

However, while we are indeed mature adults, there are some parts of us that do not grow up. Let us take a familiar example. A small child is frightened when a playful puppy barks and jumps on him. Thirty years later, as an intelligent adult (perhaps even with a Ph.D.), he sees a dog ahead of him as he walks outdoors. He has a feeling of panic and freezes in his steps. If you were to ask him, he would tell you that he knows this little dog could not possibly harm him, but this knowledge does not prevent him from being frightened. The reason for this is that the *knowledge* is in his adult mind and he is conscious of it. The *feeling*, however, is the fear experienced in childhood which resides in the subconscious mind, and is unaffected by conscious intellect. Many things that reside in the subconscious are not subject to logic. Just as an intelligent adult may have no control over his fear of dogs, we may not have control over many things that reside in our subconscious mind.

When a person *feels* he is in danger, there are a number of things that automatically take place in his body. This occurs even if he *knows* logically that he is no danger, because the body responds to the *feeling*. The mature adult who sees a dog coming his way *feels* that he is in danger of being attacked.

The body has a built-in defense reaction when it feels it is being attacked. It goes into a mode for survival, to either flee from the attacker or to fight it off. This is referred to as the "fight or flight" reaction. It is an automatic response, triggered by a feeling of danger. The major changes are an increase in heart rate, respiration and blood pressure. The blood is shifted from internal organs to the muscles, and is drawn away from the skin (the pallor of fear). The liver discharges glucose into the blood, and the adrenal glands secrete adrenaline and corticosteroids into the bloodstream. These and other physiological changes prepare a person to more efficiently fight or flee.

The mature adult who is frightened by the dog undergoes these changes because his subconscious mind senses a danger. The same type of reaction may occur when one is called into the boss' office for a reprimand. The subconscious may equate this with a physical attack and act accordingly, even though the physiologic changes in this case are grossly illogical and inappropriate. One is not going to fight the boss nor run away. However, the subconscious is not affected by logic.

It should be evident that many things can trigger a "fight or flight" reaction, even if there is no logical reason for it. For example, a husband and wife agree to meet at a certain place at a given time. He is a bit delayed, and does not show up until 10 minutes after the specified time. He finds his wife a nervous wreck, who angrily shouts at him, "Why didn't you call me when you knew you were going to be late? That's what we have the cell phones for. Don't you care at all about how I feel?"

The husband responds with equal anger, feeling the blood rushing to his head. "For heavens sake! I was delayed by traffic for 10 whole minutes. I didn't come late on purpose. Haven't you ever heard of a traffic jam? It's not like I kept you waiting for an hour."

What neither of the two recognizes is that they are reacting with subconscious feelings. When the wife was 4, she was separated from her mother in a department store, and although her mother eventually found her, the fright and feeling of abandonment remained in the subconscious, and was reawakened when the husband was a mere few minutes late. Logically, the woman could have been aware that something might have delayed the husband. In fact, if logic had prevailed, she would have called him on the cell phone. But logic did not prevail. Instead, emotion took over, an emotion that had been stored for years in the subconscious mind and was now resurrected, setting in motion the "fight-or-flight" reaction on perception of danger.

The husband's angry response was due to an old emotion being triggered. His father had once humiliated him by shouting at him in front of others. The wife's scolding triggered the painful feeling of humiliation that had been buried in his subconscious mind, which perceived her angry words as an attack, precipitating a "fight-or-flight" reaction.

If we are aware of our propensity to react to a situation because our subconscious mind may perceive things as a danger or as an attack, we may be able to teach ourselves to exercise restraint when we feel a surge of emotion. It's like counting to ten before responding to a provocation. All that is needed is a moment's delay, which gives the intellect an opportunity to operate. Instead of an angry response provoking anger and setting a vicious cycle into motion, a potentially explosive situation may be defused.

Suppose the husband, upon seeing his wife's reaction, could have marshaled the restraint and said, "I'm sorry. I assumed you would figure there was a traffic jam. I didn't think you would worry because I was just a few minutes late. Also, if you were worried you could have called me on my cell." It's very likely that the wife might respond, "I'm sorry I shouted. I guess I could have called, but I panicked. That's how I am, so next time if you see you may be late, just call me." They could then have gone on in a calm mood rather than fuming at each other.

Not every feeling of pain evokes an angry response. Suppose that you had overstayed your exposure to the sun and your back has a severe sunburn. A friend approaches you and gives you a friendly pat on the back which causes you a stinging pain. In absence of sunburn, a blow to the back that could cause such severe pain could only have been a hostile punch. However, because you are aware of the exquisite sensitivity of your sunburned skin, you do not interpret your friend's action as an attack and you do not strike out at him. Rather, you say, "Ouch! Please be careful. My back is on fire and every touch hurts," to which your friend responds, "Oops! I'm sorry."

While we are aware of the sensitivity of sunburned skin, we may not be aware of the sensitivity of our emotions, particularly of what may be going on in our subconscious mind. We are, therefore, likely to react to pain resulting from another person's actions or words as if it were from a hostile attack. If we consider that we may have "emotional sunburn" of whose presence we are unaware, we have a better chance of avoiding an angry knee-jerk response.

There are some days when "Murphy's Law" seems to be in full swing. (Murphy's Law: Anything that can go wrong, will go wrong.) Nothing seems to go right, and our nerves are frazzled. We may be so edgy that the slightest thing may be the proverbial straw that broke the camel's back, and we may snap out. Afterwards we regret our behavior, but some sharp words may not easily be forgotten. Therefore, when you feel edgy, try to keep quiet. Tell your spouse, "I'm all wound up now. It'll pass, but just bear with me a while." By the same token, if you see that your spouse is very edgy, you may say, "I'm sorry you feel that way. Is there anything I can do?" If your spouse says, "No. Please go away and leave me alone," do not become offended. It is not intended as a rejection.

My mother used to refer to the "*heilige al tadin*," by which she meant Hillel's statement in *Ethics of the Fathers* (2:5), "Do not judge your fellow until you have reached his place." She considered this an especially holy teaching because it can avoid many unjustified and distorted reactions. Living according to Hillel's principle can help prevent loss of control.

The Part Does *Not* Equal the Whole

You may be wondering, "What in the world does he mean by that?"

Let me share with you a bit of psychologic information. Our mind has two components, the "conscious mind" and the "subconscious mind." Although they coexist, they are as different from each other as light is from darkness. We will refer to this several times in this book.

The conscious mind is the rational mind, which thinks logically. We do most of our thinking with the conscious mind. Consciously, we know that a sleeve is not a suit and that a wheel is not a car. We would not try to wear a sleeve or drive a wheel. That would be insane. The past is the past and is not the present. Someone who has been gone for the past twenty years is not here today. The conscious mind tests reality.

The subconscious mind is altogether different. It operates by its own set of rules which are neither rational nor logical. In the subconscious mind, the past can exist right along with the present. To the subconscious mind, a sleeve may be a suit and a wheel may be a car. The subconscious mind is not concerned with reality.

You may say, "That is absurd!" and you are absolutely correct. However, it is the *conscious* mind that identifies and rejects absurdities. The subconscious mind is perfectly comfortable with the most far-out absurdities.

Have you ever had a dream which was just "crazy"? Dreams are produced by the subconscious mind, which tolerates "crazy" things very well. Dreams can be totally illogical and senseless.

Although we think we act logically according to our conscious mind, the fact is that the irrational, subconscious mind can exert great influence on our thoughts and actions. In fact, that all-important component of our psyche, our *emotions*, may be influenced by the irrational subconscious mind more than by the rational conscious mind. That is why our feelings sometimes do not make sense. The subconscious mind, which is probably where most of our emotions reside, does not care that things do not make sense.

One of the "absurd" ways in which the subconscious operates is that it *equates the part with the whole.* This is why the subconscious can think of a sleeve as a suit or a wheel as a car.

Have you ever met someone for the first time, and before he says or does anything, you feel a dislike for him? This feeling cannot be based on reality, because the person has not said or done anything to arouse any feelings. The reason for this feeling is that there is something—anything—about this person that is similar to a person whom you disliked in the past, even years ago. It may be something trivial, like the way his hair is combed. Logically, this is certainly no reason for disliking him. However, the subconscious ignores logic. Rather, because this person's hairstyle is similar to the hairstyle of someone you disliked, the subconscious equates and identifies the two. To the subconscious, this new person *is* the person whom you disliked, and because most feelings arise in the subconscious, you find yourself disliking this person for no apparent reason; i.e., for no reason that is apparent to the conscious mind. The reason is very apparent to the subconscious mind.

You can see what the impact of this phenomenon can be on relationships. Assume that a young woman, for whatever reasons, felt resentments against her father. Her husband happens to have a mannerism, say, he holds his knife and fork, the same way her father did. Her unconscious, operating according to its illogical rule that the part equals the whole, equates the husband with her father, and she finds herself feeling resentments against her husband.

We don't like to think of ourselves as being irrational. Therefore, when we have a feeling whose origin is in the subconscious mind, we may not say, "This feeling is absurd." Instead, we may look for a reason to justify the way we feel. The wife may conjure up a reason why she resents the husband, and she will believe that the reason is valid.

The same thing, of course, can happen with the young man, who may have felt resentments toward his mother because she had nagged him. His wife has the same color eyes his mother did. Zap! That is enough reason for his subconscious mind to transfer the feelings he had toward his mother to his wife, who may never nag him. Yet, because he feels a resentment toward her, he may interpret an innocent comment as being nagging.

So what can we do about it? Inasmuch as we do have logical thinking, we can utilize our capacity for rational thought. We do not wish to be misled and have our behavior determined by the "crazy" subconscious. When we become aware of a negative feeling, we should pause and think, "Are there, in fact, grounds for the way I feel?" and not be taken in by ascribing our feelings to something in order to justify them. If we are on the alert and realize that unrealistic and unwarranted feelings may be generated by the subconscious, we can defend and protect ourselves from such emotional carryovers that may subvert a relationship.

*R*osa's father was a hypochondriac who controlled the family with his many physical complaints. Rosa knew one thing for sure: she would never marry a hypochondriac. Several months after the wedding, Tzvi complained of severe neck pain. Rosa froze. This was precisely what she dreaded. Her husband was a hypochondriac. She consulted her rabbi about what she should do, and the rabbi assured her that people *do* get stiff necks and that she was needlessly panicking. He told her to come back after a month and report how things were going. A month later she told the rabbi that Tzvi was feeling fine and she realized that she had overreacted.

Rosa did the right thing. She took her concern to a person who could be objective and was not influenced by her early experiences. Proper guidance can avoid unwarranted reactions.

Rambam: The Supreme Marriage Counselor

*I*n the yeshivah, we are taught how to learn Rambam. This incomparable Torah scholar is the pillar of halachah. We are taught to be most perspicacious in studying his great work, giving close attention to even the slightest nuance. *How* Rambam states something is as significant as *what* he says.

In discussing the marriage relationship, Rambam cites the Talmud's statement that "a husband should love his wife as himself and should respect her even more than himself" (*Yevamos* 62b). However, Rambam makes a subtle yet phenomenal change: *he reverses the order*, saying that "a husband should respect his wife even more than himself and should love her as himself" (*Hilchos Ishus* 15:19). Why does the Rambam change the sequence of the Talmudic text, placing respect before love?

It is not an overstatement to say that understanding and observing this ruling of the Rambam could prevent perhaps the majority of marriage problems.

First, loving another person as much as you love yourself is not easily achieved. We begin life with self-centeredness. As infants, we want our parents to gratify all our needs. It is only as we mature and learn proper values that we develop consideration for others. Even so, the core of self-centeredness may not be totally overcome. Hillel interpreted the Torah commandment, "Love your fellow as you do yourself" (*Leviticus* 19:18) to mean, "Do not do to another person what you would not want done to you" *(Shabbos* 31a). The average person cannot be expected to actually love someone else as much as himself. This is a level of spirituality achieved by great *tzaddikim*, and it is too much to ask of the average person. The Torah commandments are not directed solely at *tzaddikim*. Hillel, therefore, said that what the Torah requires is for us to refrain from doing to others something that we would not want done to ourselves. That is within everyone's ability.

The halachah regarding the marriage relationship begins from the very first day. How can a person be commanded to immediately love a spouse as much as oneself? Whether the *chassan* and *kallah* had many or few contacts during their engagement, it is simply unrealistic to demand that the husband immediately love his wife as much as himself. He hardly knows her yet. Affection develops over a period of time. Furthermore, how can you legislate emotion?

Rambam, therefore, reverses the order of the Talmud. *Begin with showing your wife great respect.* That is a behavior that you can institute from day one. Rambam says: Speak respectfully to her. Do not raise your voice to her. Be gentle.

Rambam is not disagreeing with the Talmud. The Talmud places love first because that is the ultimate goal. Rambam, as a codifier of halachah, is practical. Respect is something you can initiate immediately.

Students of Rambam will note that he dictates the appropriate behavior of spouses to each other, but begins with the way a husband should relate to his wife—with respect, love, gentleness and consideration. He then goes on to describe the way a wife should relate to her husband, respecting him as if he were a king. But note! He places the halachah regarding the husband's behavior *first.* The Rambam appears to be saying that the husband is obligated to initiate the behavior that will lead to a mutually loving and respectful relationship.

There is an even more profound teaching in this Rambam ruling. By placing respect before love, Rambam is telling us how true love can be achieved. The Torah concept of love is far different from the secular concept.

*T*he latter concept of love is illustrated by the comment of R' Mendel of Kotzk, who saw a young man enjoying a tasty dish of fish.

"Why are you eating the fish, young man?" R' Mendel asked.

Rather surprised by the question, the young man responded, "Because I love fish, that's why."

R' Mendel said, "And is it because of your love for the fish that you took it out of the water, killed it and cooked it? There is nothing wrong with enjoying fish," R' Mendel said, "but don't fool yourself. You do *not* love fish. *You love yourself* and you wish to satisfy your desires. It is out of self-love that you killed and cooked the fish."

The prevailing romantic concept of love in modern society is really self-love. The other person is a vehicle whereby one satisfies one's needs. True love for another person is not "fish love." *True love can develop when one shows respect for another person,* seeks to fulfill the other person's needs and is cautious not to offend them. By putting the other person first, a person can develop true love. It is unrealistic to expect this on the very first day. Therefore, Rambam reverses the sequence. Begin with respect; love will follow.

Recognizing the wife's fine attributes, her *yiras Shamayim*, kindness, talents as a *baalabusta* (homemaking abilities) and the various other skills she has, generates respect

Prior to the *chuppah*, the *chassan* is approached to make a *kinyan* (an act binding a transaction), whereby he obligates himself to all the terms of the *kesubah* (marriage contract). It is then read at the *chuppah*, but because it is in Aramaic and *pro forma*, no one pays much heed to its content. In the *kesubah*, the *chassan* pledges himself to "work for, support and *honor*" his wife. This pledge may well have the status of a vow. A husband should be aware that saying anything demeaning to his wife may be a violation of a *neder* (solemn promise), which is a sin of awesome gravity.

There is even more depth to the remarkable statement of the Rambam. Requiring a person to love another as oneself has a pitfall. What if a person does not love himself? In most of my books I emphasize the problem of low self-esteem because it is so prevalent. People with low self-esteem do *not* like themselves very much. In such cases, loving the other person as oneself may not be conducive to a happy marriage.

I must digress a moment to define "self-esteem." It does not mean self-centeredness or vanity. To the contrary, it is just the opposite. Self-esteem means having an accurate self-perception, whereby a person is aware of all his/her character strengths as well as character defects. The knowledge of one's strengths enables a person to be productive and to correct his/her character defects. R' Yeruchem Levovitz stated this very clearly. "Woe to a person who is not aware of his character defects, but even far greater woe to the person who is not aware of his character strengths, for he lacks the ability to rectify his defects" (*L'Anavim Yitein Chein*, p. 164).

It is important to develop a healthy self-esteem. People who have negative self-images are likely to believe that everyone sees them as negative entities, and they may relate to other people on this assumption. People with low self-esteem may develop one or more behavior patterns to relieve the unpleasant sensation of being inferior. Here are some of the symptoms of low self esteem:

- a tendency to withdraw from people in anticipation of rejection

- doing things which precipitate rejection

- being a "people-pleaser," doing things for others to buy their affection or approval

- oversensitivity to criticism

- difficulty with intimacy

- boasting, name-dropping

- morbid expectations

- trying to control others

- being hypercritical of others

- fear of happiness

- fear of failure

- depression

- addictions

- eating disorders

- a variety of psychosomatic disorders

- abusive behavior

- dependency

*A*n example of how low self-esteem can undermine a marriage is the case of Yonah and Rachel, who consulted me six months into their marriage. Whereas they had a very exciting courtship and felt that they were perfectly suited for each other, they began to feel something was wrong during the first few months. Yonah was distancing himself, staying late at the office, and even when home, seemed to want to avoid close contact.

Yonah was a brilliant young man, with a Ph.D. in physics. He was very knowledgeable, and could enchant people with his brilliance. However, as I pointed out in *Angels Don't Leave Footprints*, people who are most gifted may suffer from very low self-esteem. They know they are very competent in their field of expertise, but they do not think much of themselves *as a person.*

This was the case with Yonah. He knew he was an excellent physicist and well-versed in science as a whole. However, he did not think much of himself *as a person.* Consequently, he had serious doubts that anyone could really love him. After all, one loves *a person*, not a scientific robot.

During their courtship, Yonah felt comfortable with Rachel, because for short periods of time, he knew he could impress her. However, once they were married, it was a different story.

They would now be in close contact for extended periods of time, and his façade of brilliance could not last forever. Yonah felt that sooner or later, Rachel would see through his act, and when she discovered the *person*, rather than the brilliant scientist, she would "fall out of love" with him, because there was nothing one could like about him as a person. To avoid this, he began distancing himself from Rachel, who interpreted his avoidance as his loss of love for her.

Their relationship was headed for the rocks. Having diagnosed the problem, I explained to them that they were both misperceiving things. Yonah entered treatment for self-esteem improvement, and Rachel, who knew that Yonah was really a wonderful person, was able to be supportive of him. She was able to understand that his distancing was not because he did not love her, but because he feared being rejected. As Yonah's self-awareness increased, he was able to see himself as a lovable person, and they were able to enjoy a happy marriage.

Another marriage was in danger of breaking-up because of low self-esteem.

*N*ancy consulted me because she could not understand the abrupt change in her husband's demeanor. "If he keeps this up, I don't see how I can live with him."

Ed was a successful home builder. Nancy was a housewife, taking care of the home and their four children. When the youngest child began attending school all day, Nancy found herself with time on her hands. She took a course and obtained a realtor's license. Ed thought this was a great idea, because it would fit right in with his construction business.

Once Nancy began making some sales, Ed underwent a radical behavioral change, objecting strenuously to her activities. If she wanted to show a home in the evening, Ed would say, "You can't go out at night. It's not safe." If she wanted to show a home on Sunday, he would say, "Sunday is when you should spend time with the children." He became very irritable and critical. Nancy could not understand what had happened to him.

Ed came in for an interview, and it became evident that he was suffering from a very low self-esteem, doubting that he was a lovable person. The reason that Nancy was staying with him, he felt, was because he provided well for the family. However, if Nancy were to succeed in becoming financially independent, she might decide to leave him. He felt very threatened by Nancy's business venture.

Ed entered a therapy group that was oriented to self-esteem improvement. As he began to feel better about himself, his irrational fears that Nancy would leave him abated, and he was able to actually be supportive of her career as a realtor.

Self-appreciation, in terms of having a valid self-image, is not *ga'avah* (vanity). In fact, a positive self-image is the greatest deterrent to wrongdoing. When I was a child, my father would chastise me for doing something wrong by saying, "*Es past nisht* (it doesn't become you). I was not told that I was bad, but rather that I was too good to be doing something inappropriate. A person with self-esteem will not engage in any behavior that is beneath his dignity, and will be motivated to improve upon his character defects. This is a commendable type of self-love, and if a person cares for himself in this way, he can fulfill the mitzvah of "Love your fellow as you do yourself" by caring for others as he does for himself.

Rambam has recourse to the eternal truths of the Talmud. "Who is an honored person? One who honors others" (*Ethics of the Fathers* 4:1). *When you show respect to others, you develop self-respect.* By showing respect toward his wife, the husband's self-esteem is enhanced. With better self-esteem, loving her as he loves himself strengthens the marriage bond.

This single statement of the Rambam is an entire marriage manual.

How does your spouse really feel about you? You may have no idea. This was brought home to me by something in my rehabilitation center, where alcoholics and drug addicts are treated. Part of the treatment involves working with the family of the addict.

One of the therapists had a novel idea. She had the wife and children of the alcoholic or drug addict assemble a collage that expressed how they felt about the husband and father. She then put these collages up on the wall, and had the patients review them and try to pick out which one was written by their family. *No one guessed correctly!* When they were told which one was made by their family, many of the men broke down and cried. They never thought that their wives and children had such positive feelings for them.

The Torah teaches us much about self-esteem in one brief verse. When the spies that Moses sent to scout Canaan returned, they reported that the land was populated by giants. "We were like grasshoppers in our own eyes, and *so were we in their eyes*" (*Numbers* 13:33). The message is unmistakable. *The way you feel about yourself is how you think other people feel about you.*

Be considerate of yourself. Your spouse may hold you in higher esteem than you hold yourself.

Only G-d Knows

*I*n the *Ani Maamin*, the thirteen principles of faith, no Scriptural support is provided for any of the principles except for the one asserting that G-d knows a person's innermost thoughts: "He fashioned their hearts; He understands all their doings" (*Psalms* 33:15). Why is this one principle singled out? Commentaries say that this is the most difficult of all tenets of faith to accept. Apparently it is easier to accept that the dead will be resurrected rather than that G-d knows a person's thoughts.

Why, then, should a person assume that other people are mind readers? Why should a husband or wife think that the other partner knows what they want, and that there is no need to verbalize it. "You should have known." Why should he/she have known if you did not tell them?

It is true that as years progress, a husband and wife get to know each other well enough that they can generally know what the other spouse would like. But even then, there may be exceptions, and it is always wise to ask rather than to assume. Certainly, in the early years of the marriage, one should not assume.

*T*anchum was sure that Aviva would be ecstatic with the earrings he bought for her birthday. Although she thanked him, Tanchum was disappointed that she was not as enthusiastic as he had expected. Several weeks later, she said, "These earrings will always be special to me because you bought them, but I don't wear them because they're not my taste." If Tanchum had said, "I wanted to surprise you with earrings on your birthday, but I'm not sure what you like. How about your coming along with me to choose what you want?" Aviva would have been even more appreciative.

But how is a newlywed young man supposed to know this? You cannot. That is why I am writing this book.

A corollary to not guessing what the other partner wants is, "Don't assume that words mean the same thing to him/her as they do to you."

*T*he first few weeks after they were married, Ari and Dina alternated Shabbos with their respective parents. The first Shabbos they were alone, after *Havdalah*, Ari said, "Motty (his younger brother) is coming over for *Melaveh Malkah*," A bit later, when he did not see Dina around, he went up to the bedroom and found Dina in tears. "What happened?" he asked.

Dina cried, "You didn't tell me you were inviting anyone for *Melaveh Malkah*. I didn't prepare anything. I don't have anything in the house to serve."

Ari said, "Prepare? What's there to prepare? For *Melaveh Malkah* we have a piece of challah, maybe a piece of leftover fish from Shabbos and coffee."

Dina wiped away the tears. "That's all it is?" she asked. "That's okay. I thought you have to serve like a party."

In Dina's home, when friends came for *Melaveh Malkah*, her mother served a full-course dinner. The words "*Melaveh Malkah*" meant one thing to Ari and something totally different to Dina. This resulted in her thinking that Ari was inconsiderate when he did not tell her in advance that he was inviting his brother for *Melaveh Malkah*. Ari really should have told

Dina that he was asking his brother to come for *Melaveh Malkah*, but because it seemed so trivial, he neglected to do so.

This incident, too, was not a catastrophe and was cleared up rather quickly. But sometimes the misunderstanding of words can be more troublesome. Misunderstandings can be avoided if one just asks, "What do you mean by that?" A basic rule: Ask. Don't assume.

It is important to remember that two people can look at the same thing and see it differently. We grow up in different households, often with different customs and even different values. During the early years of marriage, husbands and wives should not assume that they see things the same way. For example, some expressions that are used freely by some people may be considered improper by others.

It is important to understand that some things may have one meaning for one person and a different meaning for another. A man may feel that a new laptop computer should be a priority item in the family budget. The wife may not understand why this is so important, since there is nothing wrong with the old laptop. It may not be a question of function at all. Rather, a state-of-the-art laptop may be an ego item. Similarly, a man may not understand why the wife does not want to wear a very beautiful dress to a family wedding, simply because she has already worn it to several family affairs. Clothes can be an ego item. Spouses should try to understand why their partners value certain things. Nevertheless, even if you fail to understand why it's important, it's necessary to realize that if it's *that* important to your spouse—that should be enough reason for you to acquiese.

I cannot emphasize enough the importance of giving each other wide latitude. Do not interpret. Do not jump to conclusions. ASK, DO NOT ASSUME.

Reacting to Criticism

*L*et's face it. No one likes to be criticized. We love to hear praise, not criticism.

We all have our likes and dislikes, and what is pleasant for one person may be unpleasant for another person. Inevitably, there are going to be things which the husband may like and the wife may dislike, and vice versa. Inasmuch as the couple wishes to please one another, one has to tell the other what one dislikes, and this may be taken as a criticism.

Criticism can be constructive. Remember, G-d created woman to be *ezer kenegdo,* which is usually translated as "a helper corresponding to him." A more precise translation is "a helper *opposite* him." It would probably make for a rather boring relationship if husband and wife were identical in every way.

In one couples' group, one husband and wife claimed that they were exactly alike. They both liked the same things and never disagreed. The group thought this to be rather unrealistic and probed a bit. It turned out that they had forced an unrealistic sameness on themselves, trying to be similar in their tastes, opinions and habits. This artificiality can actually result in a strained relationship, because each partner tries to be something he/she is not. A make-believe similarity does not make for a comfortable partnership.

As noted earlier, it is the adjustment to differences that promotes personality growth. Growth may sometimes be uncomfortable. Wise grandmothers would often say, "There's nothing wrong with him. It's just growing pains."

It is only natural to wish to avoid discomfort, but discomfort may serve a function.

I once came across an article, "How Do Lobsters Grow?" Lobsters are soft animals that live inside a rigid shell. Inasmuch as the shell does not expand, how can a lobster increase its size?

The answer is that as the lobster grows, its shell becomes confining and oppressive. The lobster then retreats to an underwater rock formation where it is protected from predatory fish, sheds its shell, and produces a larger and more spacious one. Eventually, this larger shell becomes uncomfortably confining, and the lobster repeats this process several times until it reaches its maximum size.

The point to note is that the stimulus that enables the lobster to grow is *discomfort*. If not for the discomfort, the lobster would never expand its shell!

Science and technology have eliminated so many sources of discomfort that our predecessors experienced that many people think there should be no discomfort in life, and if someone is uncomfortable, there must be a pill to relieve it. We seem to have lost a tolerance for discomfort, not realizing that discomfort may be a signal to us that we should grow.

If criticism makes one feel uncomfortable (as it generally does), rather than feeling resentful one should seize the opportunity to utilize it as a stimulus for growth.

People's reaction to what they see as criticism varies. A determining factor in the reaction is the *quality of one's self-esteem*. A person with low self-esteem is apt to see all criticism as an insult and an affront to his dignity, and may react defensively or with self-denigration.

I recall having given several lectures to a class consisting of one 110 therapists. Inasmuch as they were taking the course to earn credit, they were required to submit an evaluation of the course.

One month later, I received a packet of 110 evaluations; 109 were not only very complimentary, but actually glowing with praise. However, there was one evaluation that was critical of my lectures. *I was devastated!* The lopsided score of 109 to 1 did not mitigate my distress at having been criticized. (This was in the days before I emerged from my feelings of low self-esteem. Today I am okay with a 51 percent favorable evaluation.)

If we were only aware of how helpful criticism can be, we would not take it so hard. King Solomon goes to great length to point out that wise people value criticism, and only fools are turned off by it:

"Do not admonish a scoffer, lest he hate you;
admonish a wise man, and he will love you" (*Proverbs* 9:8).
"Listen to advice and accept reprimand,
that you may grow wise in the end" (ibid. 19:20).
"The ear that hearkens to admonition may abide
among the wise" (ibid. 15:31).

Although a human being cannot achieve perfection, one can *strive* toward perfection. The colloquialism that "Experience is a hard teacher, but fools will learn no other way" is utterly wrong. Fools are those who do *not* learn from experience. It is the wise who learn from experience, and such learning often involves learning from one's mistakes.

In an inspiring essay, R' Chaim Shmulevitz cites the Talmudic comment on the verse in *Michah* (7:8), "Do not gloat over me, my foe; for although I have fallen, I have risen." The Talmud says, "Had I not fallen, I could not have risen." A fall may be the stimulus for growth and progress.

Try to think of three things that you learned from pleasant experiences. On the other hand, think of how many things you have learned from unpleasant mistakes. We should be grateful when we are apprised of having made a mistake, because that is how we grow.

Unfortunately, we often feel offended by criticism, and we may have a knee-jerk reaction, whether it is defending ourselves, retaliating, or just sulking. Any of these reactions fails to take advantage of the good that may be contained in the criticism. People who pan streams for gold may sift through tons of worthless earth just for the miniscule amount of gold they may find. Even if 99 percent of the criticism is unjustified, we would be wise to search out the 1 percent that may lead to our betterment.

Personal hygiene is very important and can obviate some criticism. You may not be aware that because you ate garlic or onions, it is not pleasant for someone to be near you. Your spouse may feel awkward in pointing this out to you, but careful attention to personal hygiene will make such comments unnecessary. It stands to reason that basic standards of cleanliness—showering, brushing your teeth, and numerous other aspects of hygiene are to be maintained at all times. Your spouse should never have cause to find you physically offensive.

Two people living in an intimate relationship can be most helpful to each other if they provide constructive criticism. This should increase their love, as Solomon says, "Admonish a wise man and he will love you." Apprising a spouse of a defect, *if it is done with sensitivity, deep care and love, will not be taken as an insult.* So, do not take offense at criticism, because this would indicate that you lack the wisdom to appreciate it.

Yaakov's younger brother became engaged, and the family celebrated at the parents' home. Lieba, Yaakov's wife, gladly extended herself and actually did most of the preparation. Several days later, in a non-confrontational tone of voice, Lieba said to Yaakov, "I was hoping you'd say something like, 'Honey, what you did was wonderful. I really appreciate your putting yourself out to make the party.' I guess I just want to know that I'm not taken for granted."

The fact is that Yaakov *did* appreciate Lieba's efforts. He just did not express his appreciation. Think about how good we feel when our efforts are recognized. If one thinks, "What can I do to make him/her happier?" we will understand that everyone needs positive strokes, and we will actually look for times when we can acknowledge appreciation.

Lieba's comment is a constructive criticism. Accepting such criticism and integrating it promotes one's character refinement. Only a fool would become defensive of such criticism.

A disciple once said to R' Yaakov Yitzchak of P'shis'che, "Someone just insulted me. He said I was lax in my *davening* and Torah study. He said that my *middos* are far from proper. He really gave me a dressing down."

The master was irritated. "How dare anyone say that about you! What did you say to him?"

The disciple responded, "I embraced and kissed him." He then drew forth the *mussar sefer*, *Reishis Chochmah*. "The author of this book criticized me sharply. I am so grateful to him for that."

Although the *Reishis Chochmah* obviously was not personally criticizing him and therefore the rebuke was easier to accept, it would be to our great benefit if we could respond to any and all on-target criticism with gratitude.

There are several rules in providing constructive criticism. First and foremost, *do not criticize when you are angry*. Criticizing when angry is likely to be interpreted as an attack, and one is apt to become defensive. Wait until the anger subsides.

A simple rule to differentiate constructive from non-constructive criticism is, "Are you willing to help the person correct the behavior which you are criticizing?" Someone who points out a defect because he is sincere in desiring the other person's betterment will be willing to be helpful. Criticizing and walking away betrays that the intent of the criticism was not benevolent.

This may sound a bit strange, but we have a precedent for it. In relating the episode of the sin of the Tree of Knowledge, the Torah states that G-d cursed Adam. "Because you listened to the voice of your wife and ate of the tree about which I commanded you saying 'You shall not eat of it,' accursed is the ground because of you; through suffering shall you eat of it all the days of your life. Thorns and thistles shall it sprout for you, and you shall eat of the herb of the field. By the sweat of your brow shall you eat bread until you return to the ground from which you were taken: For you are dust, and to dust you shall return" *(Genesis* 3:17-19).

One would think that hearing these harsh words, which condemned him to a life of hardship rather than the bliss of the Garden of Eden, Adam would have turned upon Eve and angrily berated her for enticing him to sin. But what does the Torah say immediately following the Divine chastisement? "The man called his wife's name Eve, because she was the mother of all the living" (ibid. v. 20). Instead of focusing on her misdeed, Adam said something commendatory to her: she was the mother of mankind. Adam's first reaction was to find something complimentary that he could say to her.

We can learn so much from this compliment! True, by enticing Adam to eat from the forbidden fruit, Eve condemned him to a life of toil. But Adam did not allow his self-pity to extinguish or smother his tender feelings and consideration for his wife. Rather than call her to account for his personal plight and trigger an inevitable fight, Adam related to *her* personal plight, her impending pain of motherhood.

The Midrash provides a precious insight. After seeing all the animals in pairs, Adam said to G-d, "Every living creature has a mate, but I have none," and only then did G-d create Eve.

Why did He not create Eve earlier? Because G-d knew that Adam was destined to be upset with her, and He therefore waited until Adam realized how much he needed her. This awareness would enable him to suppress his anger (*Bereishis Rabbah* 17).

If a husband recognizes that like our forefather, Adam, one should be an *adam*, a real *mentsch* and a whole person, then one's tender feelings can obliterate anger. We may assume that Adam, as the father of *teshuvah* (*Eruvin* 18b), provided Eve with guidance to rectify her transgression. And we may imagine how she accepted his reproof when she remembered his consideration and caring for her when, as a result of her act, their lives were at mortal risk.

If only we followed in the footsteps of our first father, how much grief could be eliminated! Even when criticism is warranted, find something positive to say to your spouse before criticizing him/her.

If you must criticize, be specific and point out the *behavior* which you disapprove, but do not attack the *person.* Suppose the wife wants the husband to bring up a table from the basement, but discovers that he had not done so and is relaxing on the couch. Appropriate: "Could you please bring up the table? I need it now to set up for the company." Inappropriate: "You're so lazy. Why can't you do things when I ask you?" Or, the husband may say, "I really wish you would not let the dishes stay in the sink overnight," rather than "You're a messy housekeeper." Derogatory terms like "you're stupid" or "you're so inefficient" should never be used.

(Incidentally, if it bothers you that much, why don't you wash the dishes yourself? A young man complained to his Rosh Yeshivah that his wife was a messy housekeeper. The following morning the Rosh Yeshivah came to the young man's home, took a broom, and showed him how to sweep the floor.)

The Talmud is unusually harsh with someone who humiliates a person publicly, saying that he loses his share in the World to Come, a more severe consequence than transgressing a Scriptural prohibition. The Chafetz Chaim says that it is also a grave sin to humiliate someone even in privacy.

The reason we cover the *challah* Friday night is because halachah states that the *berachah* for bread takes precedence over the *berachah* for wine. Inasmuch as we use wine for *Kiddush* before we eat the *challah*, the *challah* would be "humiliated" because it was passed over. Therefore, we protect the *challah* from being shamed by covering it.

Obviously, *challah* cannot feel and cannot be humiliated. By requiring us to cover the *challah*, our sages wished to heighten our sensitivity to people's feelings. People *do* feel, and we should assiduously avoid humiliating them, even in privacy.

In addition, specify the *incident* of which you disapprove, rather than saying "You always" or "You never." For example, "Honey, next time let's discuss major purchases in advance. I like to see what Consumers Report has to say. It's possible that other models have features we would enjoy," rather than, "You always buy things without consulting me," or "You never do adequate research." "You always" or "You never" indicate a long-standing character flaw. It is much easier to correct a single act than a lifelong trait.

We criticize when something was done or not done against our wishes. This results in an emotional state which may cause a person to say something one will later regret. An emotional rather than rational reaction actually diminishes the desired purpose of the criticism. When you must criticize, do so with your intellect rather than with your emotion.

What if your spouse does not follow these rules and criticizes in anger or generalizes or attacks you as a person rather than the behavior? *Don't respond accordingly.* Two wrongs do not make one right. Wait it out, and when everyone has cooled down, say, "Honey, I heard your criticism. I want to be corrected when I'm wrong, but when you do so in anger, I get defensive and may not hear the message."

People may think that teasing is cute. However, something said in intended good humor may touch a raw nerve and actually cause emotional pain. My suggestion: do not tease, ever.

The Talmud recognizes the emotional sensitivity of women, and Maharal states that particularly because the husband is generally the dominant person in the home, he must be extremely wary of his wife's sensitivities (*Nesivos Olam, Ahavas Rei'a* 2). Rav states that a husband should be most cautious not to irritate his wife, because a woman is emotionally sensitive and is easily moved to tears (*Bava Metzia* 59a).

Although a woman may be more sensitive emotionally, men certainly have their sensitivities. Being considerate of each other's sensitivities contributes greatly to a happy marriage.

Control

My dear newlyweds. If I had to choose one issue that is ruinous to a healthy and happy relationship, I would choose "control."

Controlling behavior is prevalent in many relationships, and is virtually always destructive. However, in a marriage, the attempt by one spouse to control the other can be absolutely devastating. Keep this principle in mind: *Control breeds resentment, not love.*

An otherwise loving relationship can be destroyed by control.

No one likes to be controlled. If a person submits to control, it is because he/she is in fear of the controlling person. Fear and love are incompatible. *If you want someone to love you, do not attempt to control them.*

Control can occur in a variety of ways. Very often, controlling people are unaware that they are controlling. Control not only ruins the husband-wife relationship, but may also have a detrimental effect on the children. Control produces tension, and growing up in a tense and controlling environment can leave deep emotional scars. This is why it is important, at the very beginning of your marriage, to evaluate whether you have controlling tendencies.

Control can occur in either direction, but given the prevailing male dominance in our society, the husband is more frequently the controller. His efforts to control may begin with as logically sounding a statement as, "Whatever transpires between the two of us must remain with us. Bringing parents into our relationship invites meddling." There is nothing wrong with this statement. A young couple *should* make every attempt to work things out by themselves. But if the husband goes beyond this and unreasonably restricts his wife's contact with her family, that may be a way of control.

Perhaps a husband may say, "Why do you have to run home every week? You're no longer an infant depending on parents. You're a married woman." A husband should understand that, especially early in the marriage, a young woman may wish to have extensive contact with her parents. If he says, "I wish you wouldn't talk to your mother on the phone so often. She puts nutty ideas into your head. I can tell when you've talked to your mother," that may be a maneuver to detach the wife from a support system so that he can wield his power over her. A further restriction may be, "I don't like the friends you associate with. They're not proper friends for you." The more he isolates his wife, the more absolute his power and control may become.

That is what control is all about: *an assertion of power*. The reasons why a person may wish to wield power over another person can be hypothesized, but as far as the couple is concerned, are of little relevance. The important point is that power and control are extremely detrimental to a marriage.

Money is often used as a method of control. The husband may deny the wife a credit card, arguing that buying on credit with its high interest rate is a sure way to get mired in deep debt. He may discourage her from signing checks, because two people on the same account may result in confusion about the bank balance, and since there is not enough money to justify a separate account for the wife, her access to money is only what he gives her. He may assure her that he will give her ample money for all her needs and may indeed do so, but his sole access to the family's money gives him another instrument of control.

Restricting the wife's access to money is a frank violation of the conditions of the *tenaim* (articles of engagement), which states that husband and wife shall have equal control of their money.

Severe emotional reactions or intense anger outbursts may cause the wife to "walk on eggs" for fear that displeasing him in any way may precipitate an unpleasant reaction. Essentially, the wife lives in fear of her husband. As pointed out above, fear and love are not compatible.

Although male dominance is more common, it is also possible that the wife may be a controller, sometimes because she is a much stronger personality than the husband, or because her father is substantially supporting the newlyweds. The latter situation may give her a feeling of power.

A husband may claim that the Torah gives him a right to control, citing the verse where G-d said to Eve, "and he shall rule over you" (*Genesis* 3:16). Torah-observant Jews accept the Talmudic interpretation of Scripture, and as Rashi points out, the "rule over you" is limited and specific. In *Bereishis Rabbah* (20), R' Yose states that this verse is not to be taken as giving a husband comprehensive control of the wife. As was noted earlier, the Talmud and halachic authorities describe proper husband-wife relations. Rambam specifies that the husband "should speak gently to his wife, not impose fear, and not be angry or tense with her" (*Hilchos Ishus* 15:19).

Rabbi Chaim Vital writes that a person's *middos* (character traits) are judged *solely* on the basis of his conduct toward his wife. A person who did much *chesed*, giving *tzedakah*, visiting the sick, consoling the bereaved and gladdening the hearts of a *chassan* and *kallah*, will certainly anticipate much heavenly reward for his many meritorious deeds.

However, one may be certain that in heaven they investigate how he related toward his wife. If he always acted with chesed toward her, he will indeed merit great reward. However, if he provoked or neglected his wife, expressing rage in the home, and did not share in her burden, this latter behavior will determine his judgment, and all the chesed he did with others will not be considered!" (cited by R' Y. Silberstein, *Aleinu LeShabe'ach*, vol. 1 p. 206).

The importance of being aware of controlling behavior is that it must be nipped in the bud. Controlling behavior does not let up on its own. If it is not managed properly in its early stages, it tends to progress and can have a serious effect on the relationship. If the control issue cannot be worked out between the couple, consulting a competent marriage counselor may be necessary.

In his book, *Marriage*, Rabbi Zelig Pliskin says, "The only power someone else has over you is the power you give them. Don't empower others at your own expense" (p. 265). A wife may object, "I am not giving him any power. He is the breadwinner in the family and I am dependent on him. He has control because he controls our finances." Rabbi Pliskin's statement needs only a slight change to be valid in such a case: "The only power someone else has over you is the power you *gave* him." Once someone has been empowered, it may be difficult to "dis-empower" him. That is why identifying controlling behavior at the very earliest stage is so important. It can be nipped in the bud, utilizing counseling if necessary.

You may say, "What! A marriage counselor? We've only been married for two months. We haven't had a chance to even get to know one another." True, but it is much better to resolve the control issue after two months than after five years, when there may be several children, and the control has become unbearable.

Here is a letter I received from a woman:

> *I am very distressed. We have been married for three years. My husband is a rather domineering person. We have our disagreements, but it always ends up that I have to admit I am wrong and apologize to him. It's just not true. I am not always wrong, and his insistence that I admit I was wrong and apologize is making a shmatte out of me. I'm not willing to live this way for the rest of my life.*

This is an example of control. At the very least, the wife could say, "I say that I'm right and you say that you're right. Let's discuss this with a knowledgeable, objective third party." Proper counseling could save this marriage, which the wife seems ready to give up on.

Let's look at this scenario:

HUSBAND: Since we've been back from our honeymoon, you've been back to your mother's every week, and you talk to her on the phone every day. I think that's a bit much, and I'd like you to cut back a bit.

WIFE: Cut back? Why? I've been with my mother constantly every day for the past twenty-one years. What's wrong with my seeing her once a week?

HUSBAND: You don't see me going back to my home every week. I have you, and that's all I need.

WIFE: Are you thinking that my visiting my mother is because you are not enough for me? That's ridiculous. I love you very much, and we are going to be together for the rest of our lives. Seeing my mother does not detract one bit from my love for you. You are everything I have.

HUSBAND: Okay, I guess I just want you all to myself. I realize now that that is unrealistic.

Or the conversation could go like this:

HUSBAND: Actions speak louder than words. As long as you're still running to your mother, you haven't detached yourself from her apron springs. You can't belong in two places. Marriage means that you detach from your parents and stay with your husband.

WIFE: I don't see it that way at all. A once a week visit does not make me tied to her apron strings.

HUSBAND: Then why is it so hard to give it up?

WIFE: Honey, why should we argue about this? If your position is right, then I will decrease my visits, but I don't see it that way. How about if we talk it over with someone?

Similar scenarios can occur with any other issue of control. If the husband appears adamant and refuses to consider his wife's position, she might say, "Honey, I love you very much, and I want to continue loving you as your wife. If what I think doesn't count for anything, then you're treating me like a little girl. I don't want to relate to you as a child to her daddy, but as your partner, your wife."

If the control issue is not dealt with, it may lead to frank abuse. One of the greatest difficulties is that an abuser is most often unaware that he is being abusive, and may deny it even when it is pointed out to him. In cases where there is violence, it is not unusual for the abuser to say, "See what you made me do," thereby blaming the victim for the abusive behavior.

Refusal by a husband to consider the wife's position is a red flag, and the wife would do well to discuss this issue with a knowledgeable person. She may be helped to find a way to best deal with what may be a tendency to control. Delay in obtaining consultation may allow "control" to progress to frank abuse. Early consultation and guidance from a counselor with competence in control and abuse counseling may save a marriage.

Negative Feelings

*I*n theory, there would be no negative feelings in an ideal marriage. Practically speaking, this is impossible. We should, therefore, know how to cope with negative feelings. Inasmuch as feelings constitute a very major portion of human experience, some clarification of feelings may be helpful, especially for a young couple.

You have heard it said, "You shouldn't feel like that." You might have been told as a child that your feelings were bad or wrong. Let's try to understand this.

The Torah says, "You shall not hate your brother in your heart" (*Leviticus* 19:17). Suppose this "brother" sets fire to my home or does me great harm in some other way. Is there any way I can avoid hating him? Is the Torah demanding the impossible of us? Is it possible to not feel anger and even some hatred when one is offended or aggrieved?

Initial feelings when provoked may not be under one's control. They are reflexive in nature, hence cannot be considered "good" or "bad." What we *do* with feelings is subject to control, hence that can be considered good or bad.

Solomon clarifies this: "Anger *rests* in the bosom of a fool" (*Ecclesiastes* 7:9). Although you may not be able to avoid the initial feeling of anger when provoked, you do have control of how long you wish to hold on to that anger. Solomon says that if the initial anger *stays* with you, then you are indeed foolish. We should be able to divest ourselves of anger. This is equally true of hatred. If someone seriously aggrieves us, we may feel hatred toward him, but this should be only momentary. We should learn ways by which we can divest ourselves of negative feelings.

Solomon says, "Hatred stirs up strife, but love covers up all transgressions" (*Proverbs* 10:12). Riva cites the verse, "You shall not take revenge and you shall not bear a grudge against the members of your people; you shall love your fellow as yourself—I am Hashem" (*Leviticus* 19:18), and comments that if a person were aware of G-d's intense love for him, he would be so ecstatic that he would not even feel a provocation. Imagine a person being told that the phone call for him was to inform him that he had won millions of dollars in a sweepstake. In his rush to the phone, he bumps his knee against the table. What would otherwise be felt as a sharp pain is totally ignored. The overwhelming joy at his good fortune completely eclipses the pain (Quoted in *Chiddushei HaLev*, vol. 4 p.137).

The love between husband and wife should be such that even if a negative feeling occurs, it should be no more than momentary. It should immediately be eclipsed by their love.

That negative feelings can be eclipsed was demonstrated to me by the sixty-two-year marriage of Esther Raizel and Benzion. They had rather sharp exchanges, but the positives far outweighed the negatives.

Esther Raizel lived to see many grandchildren and great-grandchildren. She was grateful to G-d for this blessing, and decided to express her gratitude to Him by saying a *kedushah* for every single one of her many descendants.

In Esther Raizel's neighborhood there were many shuls and *shtieblach*, some of which had multiple *minyanim*. Esther Raizel arose at dawn to the first early *minyan*, said a *kedushah*, then hurried to other *minyanim* where she could "catch" other *kedushahs*. When she finished these rounds, there was a later *minyan* at the first place. By attending the various *minyanim* at staggered times in the morning and again for *Minchah*, Esther Raizel was able to accumulate the requisite number of *kedusahs*.

Esther Raizel's rather unusual feelings and expression of gratitude dominated her personality, and although Benzion had his differences with her, he had great respect for her. He would proudly say, "I say only two *kedushahs* a day. My Esther Raizel says twenty-eight *kedushahs* every day." Gratitude and respect are components of love.

Rav Pam points out that a husband might come home after a vexatious day at work, and finding toys and games strewn all over the living-room floor, may say angrily, "Can't we have the living room clean, for heaven's sake!" There are childless couples who would give anything to be blessed with a living room strewn with lego pieces. If one only appreciated the gift of having a child, the annoyance of a toy- and lego-strewn living room would fade into insignificance.

Rabbi Zelig Pliskin cites a case of a husband and wife who were irritably trading blame for not having looked up the correct current address of the destination they sought. This unpleasant exchange was interrupted by a blind man (Elijah the Prophet in disguise?) who said, "Excuse me. Can you help me cross the street and walk me to the bus stop?" Having been suddenly made aware of the precious gift of eyesight with which G-d had blessed them, they ended their unproductive bickering. Thereafter, whenever they got into a similar altercation, the blind man's lesson reminded them of how blessed they were, and their gratitude eclipsed their squabble. Yes, gratitude is a component of love (*Marriage*, p. 115).

True love can prevent disagreements from becoming bitter quarrels. Commenting on the verse in *Proverbs* (10:12), R' Samson Raphael Hirsch says, "If two people have unfriendly feelings toward each other, they take offense at anything and everything between them. Harsh feelings are not the outcome of a quarrel; they are the cause of it."

The momentary negative feelings that are reflexive in nature do not cause disputes. The love that prevails preserves peace and harmony even when there are disagreements.

The Chuppah

*I*n the procession to the *chuppah*, the parents link arms with their children and lead them to the *chuppah*, then release their hold. After the ceremony is completed, the *chassan* and the *kallah* march back together.

This is not merely a ceremony. It is an important message that should be heeded. The *chuppah* marks a sharp transition. Until that time, the children "belong" to the parents, and their primary relationship is with them. After the *chuppah*, they "belong" to each other, and their primary relationship is with each other.

It is not easy for parents, who have raised and cared for their children for two decades, to abruptly have them taken from them. However, that is the way it is and that is the way it should be. The Torah states, "Therefore shall a man leave his father and mother and cleave unto his wife, and they shall be one flesh" (*Genesis* 2:24). Some people say that the parents' tears at the *chuppah* are not totally tears of joy. There is also an admixture of tears over the change of a long-standing relationship.

The children are now a unit. It should no longer be a matter of what he wants or what she wants as individuals, but of what *they*, as a single unit, want. Their privacy should be respected and they should be given the space to form a bond between themselves. Parents who do not relinquish their hold on their child are undermining the fusion of husband and wife as a unit. Children should never be put in the position of having to choose between their parents and their spouse.

Married children would be wise to consult their parents for advice, to benefit from the parents' experience in life. However, they must be free to make their own decisions. Attempts by parents to control the couple invariably have negative results. In those situations where the parents contribute to the newlyweds' support, they may think that this gives them the right to dictate to them what they should do. This is a grave error. Money should never be used as a leverage.

My father discouraged newlyweds from living in too close proximity to their parents because it threatened their privacy and facilitated parental meddling. He would quote from the Torah, which relates that when Joseph brought his father, Jacob, to Egypt, he said, "You will live in the land of Goshen, and you will be close to me" (*Genesis* 45:10). Joseph loved his father intensely, and as ruler of Egypt, he could certainly have arranged for Jacob to live near him, but he recognized that physical closeness may sometimes cause emotional distancing. Better that there be some physical separation, which may strengthen emotional closeness.

Years ago, things were different. The *shtetl* culture often required multigenerational closeness. Occupational skills were often handed down from father to son and household skills from mother to daughter. Given the often hostile outside environment, families overcame their differences to strengthen their internal bond. Comfort and safety was found within the extended family.

In today's world, independence is the sought-after goal. Young couples are caught in a psychological conflict. On one hand, they strive for independence. On the other hand, it is not easy for them to abruptly relinquish their dependence on their parents. Yet, they may resent any continuation of dependence, and they may even have some resentment against their parents upon whom they are dependent. A step in either direction may result in anxiety. Striving for independence frustrates their dependency needs, while satisfying the latter frustrates their desire for independence.

Emotions may be difficult to control. Parents who cared for their child for two decades may wonder whether the newcomer is providing sufficient care. I recall that early in my marriage I ran a fever, and a physician prescribed some medication. My father (usually the soul of discretion) called several times to check whether I was taking the medication and was drinking enough fluids. The implication was that my wife might not be looking after me adequately. Good intentions, but not good practice.

Parents should be sensitive to their children's adjustment in the marriage relationship and should avoid doing anything that may disturb this delicate process. Each set of parents should remember that there is another set of parents who have equal rights. But equal rights does *not* mean that the couple must spend the *exact* number of Shabbosim with each set of parents. Great care should be taken to avoid any contention between *mechutanim* (parents of the couple), because the couple's loyalties to their parents may cause friction between them.

Consideration of the children's emotional needs will not only enhance their adjustment, but will also result in the gain of a son and a daughter. As my mother used to say, this is acquiring a child without the distress of labor and delivery.

A plea to parents! Do not jeopardize your children's happiness by quibbling over trivia.

Rav Pam, in *Atarah LeMelech* (p. 129), bewails the occurrence of disagreement among the *mechutanim* on how to lead their children to the *chuppah*. One set of parents wishes to conduct their child to the *chuppah* together, and the other set of parents insist on their *minhag* that the two fathers conduct the *chassan* and the two mothers conduct the *kallah*. At the moment which should be a supreme moment of joy, Satan succeeds in disrupting the *simchah* and causing a dispute.

Rav Pam cites Rashi (*Numbers* 11:7) who writes that G-d says, "Look what my children are complaining about!" The parents have been fortunate to raise healthy children and have lived to see them married, and instead of being ecstatic with *nachas*, they create a turmoil about how they are going to walk a few meters! We say *siman tov u'mazal tov*, and many things are done for *siman tov* (a favorable omen). What could be a worse *siman* for the newlyweds than that there was aggravation, anger and dispute at their *chuppah*?

A similar situation occurs when a child is born, and each family wants the child named after someone on their side.

Shortly before my father died, he called us in and told us that we were not to name a child after him. When we protested, he said, "I have often had to mediate between families, because each one insisted on the right to choose a name for the child. The argument between the two sets of grandparents may cause friction between the baby's parents, because each feels a loyalty to his/her family. Instead of having pure joy at the birth of a child, the parents are subjected to aggravation.

"What kind of peace will I have if I know that a new mother is crying because a child of mine was obstinate in naming the baby after me? I do not want that kind of *kavod* (honor), and it will be no *nachas* for me."

Parents may make suggestions, but the decision on the child's name should be the couple's. Parents should respect their children's choice of a name, whether or not it meets with their preference.

I know of a case where a *shidduch* was actually broken off shortly before the wedding, and it was not the parents' fault. Rather, it was caused by the *chassan's* friends.

The *chassan* had attended a yeshivah until age 18, had many friends there and was close to his Rosh Yeshivah. He then transferred to another yeshivah, which he attended for five years, had friends there and was close to the Rosh Yeshivah there.

Three weeks before the wedding, friends from each yeshivah descended upon him, each claiming that he *must* take their Rosh Yeshivah to be the *mesader kiddushin* (the one who conducts the wedding ceremony, considered to be the primary honor). One group said that since as he grew up under the tutelage of the first Rosh Yeshivah, he is obligated to give him the honor, and failure to do so would be a humiliating ingratitude. The other group said that since he had now been five years with the second Rosh Yeshivah, he is obligated to give him the honor. Both groups of friends put pressure upon him, saying that to bypass their Rosh Yeshivah would be an unforgivable insult. They put the *chassan* under such severe stress that, believe it or not, he called off the wedding.

There may be a conflict between the two sets of parents as to whose rabbi should be given the honor. When it comes to children's happiness, devoted parents should set their own egos aside.

In-law Relationships

*I*n-law relationships that are not handled properly can wreak havoc with a marriage. It is extremely important to start off on the right foot. The Talmudic statement that "once an error takes root it is difficult to eradicate" (*Pesachim* 112a) makes it extremely important to avoid mistakes.

Most young couples have a very pleasant relationship with their in-laws. There is mutual love and respect. The parents are pleased that their child is happily married. However, there are sometimes parents who may have difficulty separating from their child.

"Judge everyone in a favorable light" (*Ethics of the Fathers* 1:6). Realize that your wife or husband was a child to his/her parents for many years. They cared for her/him from birth on, and the bonding that occurs between parent and child is extremely strong. As happy as parents are to see their children married, it is nevertheless a deprivation of a very close and meaningful relationship.

In regard to the building of the Sanctuary, the Midrash quotes G-d as saying to Israel, "I have given you my beloved daughter (the Torah). I cannot separate from her. Therefore, build Me a dwelling where I can be near her" (*Shemos Rabbah, Terumah*). Although G-d is everywhere, with or without a Sanctuary, He nevertheless pointed out that He wants a special closeness with Israel and the Torah. Parents, too, may desire a special closeness.

Remember that you have a wonderful wife or husband because their parents raised her/him, and essentially raised them for you. You should feel gratitude toward them as well as the respect that halachah requires. Positive feelings are reciprocal, as Solomon says, "Just as water reflects one's image, so does the heart of one person reflect the heart of the other" (*Proverbs* 27:19).

It is also important to realize that for many years, parents may have considered their primary purpose in life to be taking care of their children. We are familiar with the "Empty Nest Syndrome," the emotional state following the marriage of the youngest child, where some parents become depressed because they think of themselves as useless if they have no one to look after. This is not as severe when there are still younger children at home, but each child's leaving the house has an impact.

It is only natural, therefore, that parents may have some difficulty letting go. Their reaction can be greatly eased if there is a "weaning" process, i.e., not an abrupt cutoff. Both spouses should allow for a gradual separation. If a spouse wishes to visit the parents more frequently at first, this should not be opposed. If parents call once or twice every day, that should not be considered meddling. Gradually, the frequency of contact can be decreased without being traumatic to the parents.

Unfortunately, a husband or wife may misinterpret the spouse's desire to be in contact with parents as an indication that the spouse considers the marriage relationship as unsatisfying. That may be an unwarranted conclusion. Just as the parents need a weaning, the spouse may need a gradual weaning as well.

Especially in the early months of the marriage, consulting the parents can be very soothing. Ask their advice about setting up your household. If you do not agree with it, you may do as you wish, but asking them tells them that you value their opinion and that you do not wish to detach from them.

The worst thing one can do is put the spouse into a conflict of loyalty, causing them to choose between the spouse and the parents. This is a needless and destructive tug-of-war that can cause resentments on the part of everyone.

Never, but never, make any disparaging remarks about your in-laws, not even as a joke. You may think it is funny, but it may appear offensive to your spouse. Remember, halachah requires that one respect and honor not only one's parents, but also one's parents-in-law (*Yoreh Deah* 240).

Some young people are comfortable in calling their parents-in-law "Dad" or "Mom." Others are uncomfortable doing so, and they may prefer the Yiddish *shver* or *shvigger*. Calling parents-in-law (and indeed, parents) by their first name is not accepted in Torah families.

A problem may arise if a young man or young woman has been at odds with his/her parents. They may even say, "I married just to get away from them." They may want to enlist the spouse against the parents. The spouse may be caught in a no-win situation, antagonizing either the partner or the in-laws.

One woman said, "It gives my husband satisfaction to hear me vent against his parents. It enables him to vent his anger at them through me." This is not good for the couple's relationship and certainly not for the in-law relationship. If a husband has issues with his parents, the wife should encourage him to do whatever is necessary to resolve them, but not allow herself to become the vehicle for his dissatisfaction with them.

Parents may have blind spots toward their children and an attitude toward the children-in-law. This is certainly not universal. Many mothers-in-law and daughters-in-law have wonderful relationships.

However, the story goes that a woman was telling her friend about her married children.

"*I* don't have much *nachas* from my daughter-in-law," she said. "She is spoiled. My Benny has to bring her breakfast in bed. She demands that he take her out to expensive restaurants, and when they eat at home, he has to do the dishes. Oy! What kind of marriage he got himself into."

The friend said, "And is your daughter happily married?"

"Thank G-d, from my daughter I have *nachas*. Her husband is an angel. You know, he brings her breakfast in bed. He takes her out to expensive restaurants, and when they eat at home, he does the dishes for her. She is a lucky girl to have such a wonderful marriage."

Parents may not fully appreciate that the couple is now a unit, and may have a discussion with one of the spouses to the exclusion of the other, although the matter may involve or affect both. Parents may make critical remarks to their child about their spouse. If this occurs, a husband or wife should say, with a tone of voice that shows parental respect, "We will listen to what you say, but we must do so together." Each partner must not allow the spouse to be torn between loyalty to the marriage and loyalty to the parents.

Children should let their parents know that although the marriage does result in a degree of separation from them, they still love them very much and can be counted upon to be there for them if the need arises. If, however, parents damage their relationship with the couple by forcing either partner to choose between them and the spouse, it will have a negative impact on the relationship with the parents.

Brothers- and sisters-in-law may not be as possessive as parents, but they, too, may react to a sibling's marriage as if something was taken away from them. They may want to maintain a close relationship, which the spouse-in-law may consider intrusive. Patience, understanding and empathy can prevent the development of problems.

Communication

*T*wo-way radio! That's the way to go!

As noted earlier, not everything that appears to be a problem in communication is actually so. Remember the example of the two people going in opposite directions on the moving sidewalks? Even with the finest communication skills, you cannot communicate if you are not both headed in the same direction.

I was standing with a friend when he received a signal on his two-way radio. After finishing his conversation, he said, "All family members should have two-way radios and talk to each other only that way.

"When I talk to someone on my radio, it's not like talking on the telephone. He cannot interrupt me. He must wait until I finish speaking, then he can talk, and I can't interrupt him.

"Very often, when you say something to a person, instead of hearing you out, he is thinking of what to say in response, usually defensively. How can people really understand each other if they don't give the other person a chance to finish what he's saying, and if they are preparing a reply instead of listening to what he's saying?"

Although it is unrealistic to communicate via radio, we can behave "as if." One of the greatest problems in communication is not hearing what the other person is saying and consequently not having enough time to consider the merits of their point of view and think through a proper response.

There is an additional reason why one should not interrupt another person's speech. The Talmud says that one of the features of a wise person is that he does not interrupt another person's speech (*Ethics of the Fathers* 5:9). If you interrupt while your spouse is speaking, you are indicating that you lack wisdom. How can you expect your spouse to respect you if you are declaring yourself to be a fool?

The Talmud cites R' Zeira as stating that the reason for his longevity was never having raised his voice at home (*Megillah* 28b). This is not only conducive to long life, but also to a long and happy marriage. The wise King Solomon says that the words of the wise are hearkened to because they are spoken softly (*Ecclesiastes* 9:17). As soon as you raise your voice, the other person tunes you out. If you wish to be heard, speak softly.

In his book, *10 Minutes a Day to a Better Marriage*, Dr. Meir Wikler gives excellent instruction for effective communication. Rather than duplicate the information here, I suggest you go to the source. It is a book worth reading and following his directions.

There is one aspect of communications that should be borne in mind, and that is *non-verbal communications*. Let me share a personal incident with you.

*I*n my first year of psychiatric training, I had a patient who was a hypochondriac, and whose various complaints were clearly drug-seeking behavior. I told the nurse to give him a placebo injection of saline, but she told me that hospital regulations prohibit the use of placebos. This was rather strange, because as an intern in medicine, I did use placebos when I felt them to be warranted. Curious, I asked the clinical director for an explanation of this restriction.

The clinical director said, "Dr. Twerski, the human method of communication by speech is superimposed on a more primitive method, which is found in lower forms of life that do not have speech. Animals communicate in a number of ways, even by emitting a body odor. People may communicate by body language, which may be even more effective than speech. Not only are tone and inflection as significant as words, but one's facial expression and posture may be a more powerful communication than many words.

"It is important to realize that whereas we may have control over our verbal communication, we have far less control over our non-verbal communication. If you give the patient an injection, saying 'I'm giving you something for your pain,' your non-verbal communication, over which you have little control, will say, 'I'm giving you *nothing* for your pain.' This mixed message will result in your patient losing trust in you.

"In contrast to some other medical specialties that utilize technology in treatment, the most important therapeutic tool the doctor has is the patient's trust. You cannot endanger that."

Prior to learning this, although I tried to abide by the Torah prohibition on lying, I nevertheless did stretch the truth on occasion, rationalizing why it was permissible to do so. (There are few things that are abused as much as the *hetter* (permission) of *lemaan hashalom,* for the sake of peace.) Being convinced of the validity of the clinical director's words, I have stopped lying altogether, because I realized that *I am not a good liar.*

A roll of the eyes, a grimace or frown, repeatedly looking at the watch—these gestures convey your thought even more than words.

Your spouse has a built in "radar" for detecting fabricated feelings and insincere intentions.

Mutual trust is the basic cement of a successful marriage. This trust should never be put at risk. Without genuineness, the best efforts at communication will be hollow and ineffective.

With very, very rare exceptions, such as protecting the spouse from shocking news, husbands and wives should not lie to each other, even when one can justify stretching the truth. Your body language and non-verbal communication will give you away. You should make a firm commitment to each other: "I will never lie to you. If there is something I cannot tell you, I will say, 'I cannot tell you that,' and we will respect each other's confidentiality." Making such a commitment and sticking to it is far more conducive to a happy marriage than telling "white lies."

Yes, but what if the meat loaf tastes like burnt rubber? Are you supposed to hurt your wife's feelings? Of course, if you wish to compliment her and tell her that it was just delicious, you'll be eating burnt rubber meat loaf again and again. And why not? Didn't you tell her it was superb? And what if she chooses to make meat loaf for guests? That's not fair to the guests nor to her.

You might say, "Honey, I know you're trying to please me, and that's why I appreciate everything you make, and I love you for it. But there was something not right about the meat loaf, and if we serve it to company, it may not be well received. Let's look for a meat loaf recipe that will please others as well as me." I can assure you that if you say this with proper feeling, your wife will not take this as an insult. As was pointed out in the discussion of criticism, when criticism is delivered lovingly, it will not only be accepted but even appreciated.

Unfortunately, you cannot be as frank as this with other people, but try to avoid lying even to them.

I was once invited to a young couple's home for dinner, and everything the young woman served tasted so bad that I became very nauseous. I could not wait to get home so that I could regurgitate. Yet, to be polite, I told her that everything was delicious. You may be certain that I never again accepted an invitation to their home.

Inasmuch as I had told her how delicious the food was, the woman undoubtedly served it to other friends, who, like myself, now shun invitations to her home. For all I know, this woman may *never* have dinner guests again. It would have been much kinder in the long run had I said, "Esther, we enjoy your company, so please don't take offense at this. I know you tried to serve gourmet dishes, but those should be left for chefs. Stick to simple foods. I hope you'll invite us again, and if you will just serve roast chicken with potatoes instead of exotic dishes, we'll all have a great time."

Not infrequently, a spouse may try to avoid communicating by remaining silent. That is not avoidance by any means. Silence can be a very powerful communication.

In all likelihood, the reason for silence is *fear of pain.* One might feel vulnerable, thinking, "If I told you my real feelings, you might hurt me." Or, one may be fearful, "If I expressed my anger, it would destroy you." Or, "If you found out what I was really like, you might not like me."

A few moments of silence to think about an appropriate, constructive response is helpful in avoiding a knee-jerk reaction, but silence as avoidance is counterproductive. If one is going to be silent, one should offer an explanation. One might say, "I'd like to respond to you, but not just right now, okay?"

Sometimes a person's silence may be a way of willfully ignoring another person's words or actions. This is tantamount to saying, "You do not deserve a response," and can be even more belittling and insulting than harsh words.

Warm, caring and loving statements are important on their own, as well as facilitating communication. You can always think of something nice to say. Keep a positive attitude and you will notice the positives. You need not feel uncomfortable and need not have any fear of rejection. As long as your compliments are sincere they will be accepted with gratitude and love.

Do you make your husband's lunch or pack his suitcase? Put in a note, "I love you." A post-it affixed to the wife's make-up mirror reading *"Bei mir bist du schoen"* (to me you are beautiful), will be cherished forever.

Take the time to express your appreciation appropriately. When we are annoyed about something (trivial or not) we tend to enumerate every little thing that rubbed us wrong. Do the same with a compliment. Don't just say, "Thanks for bringing in the groceries from the car." Rather, say, "I was so thrilled when I went out to the car and found that you had already brought in the groceries. I know you were tired when you came home from learning last night (after a full day) so I doubly appreciate how considerate it was for you to take the time to do this for me." By spelling out our gratitude in detail, we assure our spouse of the truth of our feelings of love and caring.

Communication when one is angry is so important that it merits a chapter of its own.

Anger

*T*here is some confusion about anger, partially due to the fact that the Hebrew word for anger, *kaas*, is used for three different phases of anger, and unless these are properly defined and distinguished, the proper management of anger may be problematic.

The first phase of anger is the *feeling* one has when hurt or provoked, either physically or emotionally. This is a feeling over which a person does not have much voluntary control. It is extremely difficult to not feel angry when one is offended.

The Chafetz Chaim, who was never seen to express anger, would pray fervently that G-d relieve him of this feeling. He despised the feeling, yet because he was apparently unable to eliminate it, he asked G-d to help him not feel angry.

The second phase of anger is the *reaction* to the feeling. This may be across a broad spectrum, from very mild to very severe. A person may walk away without making any response. He may reply verbally, in a normal tone of voice or very loudly. He may insult the other person, or may strike back at him physically. A person *does* have control over this phase. Restraint may require effort, but a person can decide how he will respond to a provocation.

As noted, the Hebrew word *kaas* is used for both phases, the initial feeling and the reaction. Because *kaas* is considered as grave a sin as *avodah zarah* (idolatry), people may have much guilt over having *felt* anger. It is clear, however, that what the Talmud equates with *avodah zarah* is not the initial *feeling* of anger, but the reaction of rage. The Talmud says, "If one tears his clothes in anger, it is as if he worshiped idols" *(Shabbos 108b)*. This is the source of Rambam's statement that *kaas* is as grave a sin as *avodah zarah*.

Because the way we act strongly impacts our feelings, it is possible that by completely controlling one's response and avoiding any aggressive reaction to provocation, one may insulate oneself to the point where one may not feel angry. However, this is something achievable only at a very high level of spirituality.

*I*t is related that when the *ger tzedek* (righteous proselyte) of Vilna was about to be burned at the stake for converting to Judaism, the executioner said, "I suppose you are thinking that after you are in heaven, you will bring down the wrath of G-d upon me."

The *ger tzedek* replied, "When I was a child, I had some toy soldiers. A playmate of mine broke some of them, and I was very angry at him. I asked my father, who was the ruler of our area, to punish him, but my father ignored my request. I thought, 'Just wait until I grow up and have the power my father has. Then I will punish him.'

"When I grew up and came to power, the incident of my childhood was a meaningless trifle, and of course, I did not punish my childhood playmate.

"When I will be in the Eternal World, I will realize how insignificant this human body is. I will have no intention of punishing anyone for destroying it."

It is possible to put things in proper perspective, so that some personal offenses are seen as relative trivia that are not worth making a fuss over.

Some misguided psychologists have suggested that a person should "discharge" his anger by breaking or hitting things. Not only is this forbidden by the Talmud, but also has no basis in psychology. Rage does not eliminate anger. To the contrary, it may aggravate it.

On the other hand, people who have not reached the spiritual level where they do not feel angry when provoked may eliminate the conscious awareness of anger by "repression."

Repression is a subconscious process whereby the mind blocks the awareness of something, if being aware of it is too threatening to a person. If someone believes that the *feeling* of anger is an abhorrent sin, or if one thinks that if he feels anger he may lose control of himself and do something rash, he may *repress* the feeling of anger. This is not something one does consciously. It is a subconscious psychological defense mechanism, and it happens automatically without one's knowledge of it.

The problem is that a repressed feeling is not eliminated. Rather, it lies buried in the subconscious mind from which it may exert negative effects on one's emotions and behavior.

In order to pray, as the Chafetz Chaim did, for G-d to remove the feeling of anger, or to reach a spiritual level where one does not feel anger, one must be aware that one indeed has the feeling of anger. If anger is repressed so that one is unaware of having it, one cannot pray for G-d to remove it and cannot work toward a spiritual level where it will not be felt.

A person should, therefore, realize that the *initial feeling of anger* is quite normal, that the feeling by itself is not *avodah zarah*, and that one should try to eventually overcome it in a healthy way, by prayer and spiritual growth, but not by repression. However, inasmuch as the reaction to anger is under voluntary control, one should exert that control. Of one who restrains his reaction to anger, the Talmud says that he is beloved of G-d (*Shabbos* 88b) and that his sins are forgiven (*Yoma* 23a).

The reaction to the feeling of anger when provoked is proportionate to how annoyed or hurt one was by the provocation. As was pointed out earlier, this depends on a person's sensitivity. A person with a fragile self-esteem may feel deeply offended by a comment that would not be given much weight by someone with solid self-esteem.

The third phase of anger is *resentment*; i.e., carrying a grudge and sustaining hostile feelings. This is forbidden by the Torah: "You shall not hate your brother in your heart" (*Leviticus* 19:17). Inasmuch as the Torah does not impose impossible tasks, it is clear that although resentments are feelings rather than actions, it is possible for a person to divest himself/herself of negative feelings toward others.

It is unrealistic to think that two people, regardless of how much they love one another, are going to be able to avoid moments of anger. It is, however, possible for the anger to be managed in a way that will not affect their relationship.

Let us address "resentment" first. Managing resentments is important not only in marriage, where a lingering grudge can seriously damage the relationship, but also in any social relationship.

The Torah explicitly forbids not only taking revenge, but also not saying to anyone who has offended you and now asks a favor of you, "I will do it for you, even though you do not deserve it" (*Leviticus* 19:18). You must do the favor and keep silent. There is, therefore, no permissible way in which you can possibly act on a grudge to redress the wrong that was done to you. The person who offended you is not in any way affected by how you feel about him. *You* are the only person who is affected by the grudge. It may cause you to be in a bad mood, it may give you headaches or interfere with your digestion. By holding a grudge, *you are punishing yourself for the other person's bad behavior.* In all likelihood, the person who offended you has forgotten about the incident, yet you are still carrying the burden of its weight. Good judgment should prevail so that we do not do this to ourselves.

A recovering alcoholic who was several years sober was cruelly exploited. In relating to me what had happened to him he said, "I am full of resentments, but I will go to an Alcoholics Anonymous meeting today and try to divest myself of them. You see, if I hang on to my resentments, I will drink again." I was impressed by his awareness of something that relatively few people know: *harboring resentments is self-destructive.* This is as true for non-alcoholics as for alcoholics.

The deleterious effects on oneself of bearing a resentment in a marriage relationship are further compounded by the consequences of the discord it may cause between husband and wife. Therefore, it is important to learn to forgive one another, and to forgive *promptly*. If, in any way, one spouse has offended the other, a quick apology is in order. An excellent rule in marriage (as well as in all other relationships) is: *never defend a mistake.*

Of course, one cannot apply this rule if one does not think one has made a mistake. Even then one may say, "I didn't think that was wrong, but if it was, I stand corrected." Nor should one counter a statement such as, "It was just an oversight," with "Stop being defensive!" There are such things as rather innocent oversights, and one should not make mountains of molehills.

When you apologize for something, be sincere, not manipulative; i.e., "I said I was sorry already. Why can't you put it behind you and move on? Just forget it now." That is hardly a genuine apology. Similarly, "I'm sorry for what I said, but you have to understand that I was under a lot of stress." That is making excuses and avoiding responsibility. A more meaningful statement is, "I'm sorry. It was wrong for me to say something hurtful to you when I was stressed."

If you feel offended by your spouse, tell him/her, *in a gentle way*, how and why you feel. Your spouse may apologize or explain the behavior in a way that enables you to see it in a different light.

The Talmudic dictum, "judge everyone favorably," applies to a husband and wife as well. Even the most apparently offensive act may have an explanation.

The *tzaddik*, R' Aryeh Levin, said that he had always tried to judge others favorably, but did not realize how an act may be misinterpreted until the following incident.

R' Levin was attending a funeral, when he saw a close friend of the deceased leave the funeral procession and go over to a stand where flowerpots were sold. He bought a flowerpot and returned to the procession. R' Levin was very upset by this. Attending the funeral of a close friend is no time to be thinking about or buying flowerpots.

In keeping with the commandment, "You shall reprove your fellow and do not bear a sin because of him" (*Leviticus* 19:17), R' Levin told this man that his behavior was inappropriate.

The man said to R' Levin, "There is a patient in the hospital who has a disease so contagious that the doctors ordered that everything that was in contact with him must be burned. They were going to burn his *tefillin*, too. I pleaded with them not to burn the *tefillin*, and I promised them that I would personally see that they were buried. They acceded to my request. I bought the flowerpot in which to bury the *tefillin* at the cemetery according to halachah."

R' Levin said, "Never again will I accuse someone of any wrongdoing without giving him a chance to explain his behavior."

Regardless of how clear something may be to you, *don't jump to conclusions*. Without manifesting anger, ask for an explanation. You would want to be given the benefit of the doubt. Give this consideration to your spouse.

I am going to close the chapter on anger with a story that you may already know. It is a story that has given rise to mixed reactions, but I cite it for two reasons: (1) my father's interpretation, and (2) the central figure in the story is a revered ancestor of mine. I will convey the story exactly as I heard it from my father.

*W*hen R' Nachum of Chernobyl, author of the basic chassidic work *Meor Einayim,* died, his wife sought support from his colleagues. On one visit to the chassidic master, R' Baruch of Medzhibozh, the latter asked her, "Please tell me some of the practices of your holy husband." The Rebbetzin thought for a few moments, then abruptly rose and said, "I must leave here."

"But why?" R' Baruch asked.

"Because," the Rebbetzin said, "I knew of so many of my husband's practices, and now my mind has gone blank and I cannot think of a single one. Worse than that, I cannot envision what he looked like. I must take that as a sign that I do not belong here."

R' Baruch escorted the Rebbetzin to her coach. Just as it was about to leave, she stopped the driver and alighted. "I just thought of an incident involving my husband. Normally, I would not relate this. However, inasmuch as my mind had gone blank and this incident was the only thing that occurred to me, I take that as a sign that I am supposed to relate it to you.

"All our years, we lived in abject poverty. There were times when the children went hungry. There were times when we shivered in the cold because we could not afford wood for the fire.

"My husband had a pair of *tefillin* that were very dear to him. The parchments had been written by Ephraim the Sofer (scribe), whom the Baal Shem Tov rated along with the Biblical scribes, Ezra and Nehemiah. There was a very wealthy man in town who offered to buy the *tefillin* for 50 rubles. *Fifty rubles!* That was enough to provide for the family for two whole years! I said to my husband, 'Please, sell the *tefillin*. For 2 rubles you can get a pair of fine *tefillin*, and we will be able to feed the children.' But my husband said that the *tefillin* were not negotiable.

"I was caring for my niece, Malkele, who was orphaned from her mother. I said to my husband, 'When Malkele needs a dowry to get married, will you then sell the *tefillin*?' My husband said that to marry off a needy girl, one may even sell a Torah scroll. That appeased me somewhat.

"One year, as Succos approached, there was not an *esrog* to be had. My husband was very saddened that he would not be able to fulfill the mitzvah of the four species. On the morning before Succos, as he returned from shul, he saw in the distance a man carrying an *esrog* and *lulav*. All excited, he ran to the man and asked him how much he wanted for the *esrog* and *lulav*. The man said, 'Rabbi, this is not within your means. It is the only *esrog* and *lulav* in the entire territory. The wealthiest man in town is paying 50 rubles for them.'

"My husband promptly said to the man, 'Just stay here, don't move.' He reasoned that he would not need the *tefillin* for the eight days of Succos, but he needed the *esrog* for Succos. He hurried to the home of the rich man, sold the *tefillin* for 50 rubles, returned to the first man and bought the *esrog* and *lulav*.

"I returned from the market, having scrounged to get a bit of food for Succos. I looked at my husband, who was ecstatic with joy. His faced radiated as if the Divine Presence had rested on him. 'Why all the joy?' I asked. He just made some small talk and avoided my question. But I continued to nag him for the reason for his joy, and he finally revealed to me how he had acquired the *esrog* and *lulav*.

"I felt my head spinning and the world turning dark. I remembered all the scenes of the children going to bed hungry and shivering from the cold, but he would not sell the *tefillin* for them, yet he sold them to acquire a fruit which would be worthless in seven days! And worst of all, where would I get a dowry for Malkele?

"I demanded, 'Where is the *esrog?*,' and my husband pointed to the cupboard. In a fit of rage, I opened the cupboard, took out the *esrog*, and threw it on the floor, smashing it and breaking off the *pitom*.

"My husband turned pale, and tears ran down his cheeks. Then he said softly, 'My precious *tefillin* I no longer have. An *esrog* to fulfill the mitzvah of the four species, I don't have either. How Satan would rejoice if I shouted angrily at my wife and ushered in the Succos festival with my *shalom bayis* (peaceful home) in ruins. I will not grant Satan that pleasure.' "

R' Baruch of Medzhibozh said, "Rebbetzin, I can understand why your husband refused to part with the *tefillin* all those years. I can also understand why he sold the *tefillin* to acquire an *esrog* for Succos. But how a person can have the superhuman self-mastery not to react with an angry word at such a provocation, that is beyond my grasp. Only someone as holy as your husband could achieve that."

Some people see the Rebbetzin as the heroine of the story. My father obviously sided with R' Baruch at marveling at R' Nachum's extraordinary restraint. I am sure that the reason he retold this story numerous times was to impress upon us the importance of avoiding angry words.

Even if we cannot have the restraint of R' Nachum, we can certainly make an effort at avoiding expressions of rage in the home.

A *Touch* of Anger

I pointed out how important it is to understand the meaning of the first two of the *sheva berachos*. I doubt whether this is grasped by most young couples. Their fantasy of marriage is more likely to be that the other partner will make them "whole" by providing for all their emotional needs. Esther thinks that Shmuel will be the answer to her prayers, and Shmuel thinks the same of Esther.

Not too long after the wedding, Esther makes a startling discovery. Shmuel is indeed a fine young man, but is not, as she had erroneously assumed, primarily dedicated to fulfill *her* needs. Rather, he is more interested that Esther should fulfill *his* needs. A wonderful dream, a pleasant fantasy has just been shattered. Esther feels some disappointment and even a touch of anger at Shmuel for bursting her lovely fantasy balloon. Shmuel feels the same type of disappointment and anger at Esther for not living up to his fantasy. He wants to make her live up to his fantasy, and she wants to make him live up to hers. These are the seeds of a power struggle: who is going to make over whom.

This may not lead to a serious altercation, but Shmuel, discovering that although Esther is a very fine person, she falls short of fulfilling his fantasy of having all his needs satisfied, may begin to do other things that he feels are fulfilling. He may start staying at the office much longer. He may begin spending hours at his computer. He may spend more time with his friends or digesting every column in *The New York Times*. Esther may seek to fulfill herself in similar activities.

These are essentially avoidance maneuvers, and lead to a diluting of intimacy. This distancing may continue without dramatic consequences, but is also fertile ground for the development of major disagreement.

Remember how the subconscious mind may not mature along with the intellect? Some very early emotions, even those from infancy, may linger in the subconscious mind for decades. They may be resurrected by a triggering event.

An infant makes its wishes known by crying, and mother responds by fulfilling the wish. Hunger is probably the first experience of anxiety in human life. If, for whatever reason, mother delays the feeding, the infant may feel anxiety. This experience is imprinted in the subconscious as "unfulfilled needs = anxiety." When a husband or wife feel that their needs are not being fulfilled, they may experience anxiety. They may have no idea why they are feeling this way. It is a throwback to an infantile emotion residing in the subconscious mind that has now been evoked.

Shmuel's and Esther's love for each other may be affected by the emergence of this anxiety. Anxiety is akin to fear, and in some cases, the husband and wife may actually develop a low-key fear of each other, and may even avoid each other because closeness may generate the discomfort of fear. They may have no notion why they are in an avoidance pattern, because they *do* love one another.

When we experience discomfort, we generally look for a reason why we are feeling this way. Shmuel and Esther may not understand why they feel some discomfort in each other's presence, and may begin to look for reasons to explain it. Inasmuch as all human beings have some character defects, they may begin focusing on faults they can find in one another. As they do so, relatively minor defects that would otherwise go unnoticed are magnified, and may become points of contention and expressed dissatisfaction. Molehills may become mountains.

This sorry state of affairs could be prevented if young men and women divested themselves of unreasonable expectations.

Every young man and woman is entitled to a happy marriage. However, "happiness" requires careful definition. In the Declaration of Independence, the Founding Fathers were wise in citing "*pursuit of happiness*" as an inalienable human right. Note that they did not say "pursuit of *pleasure.*" They did not equate happiness with pleasure. Modern society has erred in equating the two, and if people lack the pleasure they desire, they may feel unhappy.

It is only normal for a person to desire pleasure, but its absence should not result in unhappiness. Our great works of *mussar* even talk about *simchah b'yisurim,* being happy even while experiencing suffering!

True happiness results from fulfillment of one's potential. One can be at peace, *shalom,* with oneself when one is *shalem* (whole). R' Samson Raphael Hirsch points out that the word *same'ach* (joyful) is very closely related to the word *tzame'ach* (growing); i.e., growth leads to happiness.

Think of it this way. A four-cylinder automobile than can generate only sixty horsepower will give you a much smoother ride than a car with a powerful eight-cylinder engine that has two non-functioning cylinders. Even though the latter may generate three times more horsepower than the smaller engine, the ride will be rough because of the vibrations resulting from the two non-functioning cylinders.

It is the same in life. A person with lesser potential may coast through life fairly smoothly if he is using all his potential, even though he may not be able to accomplish much. A person with much greater potential who is not utilizing all of it may have great achievements, but is likely to be quite uncomfortable *because he is not fulfilling his potential.*

Personality growth requires effort. One does not become a better person by doing nothing. We must often make sacrifices to achieve growth.

Marriage can result in true happiness because each partner can help make the other partner *shalem.* The words of the Torah are very instructive. G-d said, "*Eh'ehseh lo ezer kenegdo,* I will make for him a helper opposite him" *(Genesis* 2:18). It is precisely because husband and wife have differences and make the effort to adjust to one another that there is growth. If a husband and wife were in every way identical, there would be no need for change and consequently no growth. Without *kenegdo* (opposite to him) there is no need for adjustment.

It is by personal growth that one becomes a *mentsch*, the *adam* referred to in the *sheva berachos*. This leads to the next *berachah*, "gladden the beloved companions."

Some people think that a successful marriage depends on finding the right person. Actually, it depends much more on *being* the right person.

Properly understood, the discovery of differences in each other and the awareness that one must make adjustments to accommodate, far from producing disappointment and anger, should result in gratitude and in appreciation of the opportunity to grow, to become whole and to achieve true happiness. Remember, it is the discomfort and stress which are the catalysts to make the lobster change and grow.

Reacting to Stress

*T*here is no such thing as a stress-free existence, and there is no way one can have a stress-free marriage. Furthermore, stress has been given an unwarranted bad press. Stress is what makes the world go round. Without stress to get us moving, we would hibernate all year round like bears in the winter.

It is when stress is excessive, when stress becomes *distress*, that it becomes destructive, affecting a person physically as well as emotionally. But we should realize that the degree of stress we experience is not always justified by reality. Our perception of a situation may be distorted, and our minds and bodies may react according to our distorted perception.

For example, a person who experienced a severe trauma at some point may recover completely from its immediate effects, but may be vulnerable to recurrent feelings of anxiety even years afterward. Certain incidents may be "triggers" that resurrect the feelings experienced at the time of the trauma. This is known as Post Traumatic Stress Disorder (PTSD), and this should be treated by a competent therapist. Current situations which are not in any way a danger or a threat may be perceived as such.

Distorted perceptions may also occur when we assign undue importance to things that are relatively minor. Something unpleasant may occur which is, in fact, not a calamity, but which may be perceived as such. For example, on your way to an important appointment you have a flat tire or are hopelessly stuck on the highway because of a tractor-trailer which jackknifed and will not be removed for two hours. True, this is *very* unpleasant, but important as the appointment may be, this is not quite a catastrophe.

Here is a good rule-of-thumb for coping with stressful situations. Project yourself five or ten years in the future. When you look back on this incident, will it still loom as large, or will you dismiss it as "one of those things that happens"? Sometimes we look back at incidents which may have felt catastrophic at the time, but years later we not only dismiss them but may even laugh at them.

A very active and daring child may take a walk on the fence, fall, and fracture his forearm. Mother calls 911, then calls father at work, who rushes to meet them in the hospital emergency room. It appears to take forever for a doctor to see the child, who may be howling with pain. The anxiety at such time may be extreme.

Sixteen years later, the parents walk this son to the *chuppah*. The arm has long since healed completely. The parents are ecstatic with joy at their son's marriage. If someone were to remind them of the child's injury sixteen years later, they may laugh, saying, "That was some ordeal!" but they are hardly disturbed by that now.

*W*hen my son became Bar Mitzvah, many relatives came for the *simchah*. My wife cooked gefilte fish in advance, sealed it in jars, and because we were short of refrigerator space, I stored the jars in the shul refrigerator intending to bring them home *erev Shabbos*. When we returned from shul Friday night, my wife asked, "Where did you put the gefilte fish?" Had I been hit by a brickbat, I could not have been more shocked or crushed. I had forgotten to bring the gefilte fish home, and there was no *eruv!* There were thirty guests for the Friday night meal, and no gefilte fish. Imagine the hurt and bewilderment on my wife's face. Imagine yourself in my predicament, and you may know what I felt like.

That son now *B"H* has grandchildren, and the absence of gefilte fish at the Friday night meal was not the calamity I had envisioned it to be. Sometimes, when I think I am in a very difficult predicament, it helps to remember that few things can be as aggravating as not having the gefilte fish to serve for the guests, but it really had no lasting impact on my life.

So apply the rule. If you know that years later the incident will fade into relative insignificance, *don't overreact to it as a catastrophe.* Keep yourself level-headed and do whatever can be done to cope optimally with the current situation.

Husbands and wives can be of immense support to each other. For example, the husband may return home from work all tied in knots because a lucrative contract that he was working on was given to a competitor. This is an ego blow as well as a financial loss, and the insult to the ego may inflate the incident into humongous proportions. The wife, who is unaffected by the ego factor, may be able to comfort and reassure the husband. "Honey, you tried your best. You gave it all you've got. The other guy may have under-bid you or perhaps used some pull to land the contract. I'm proud of you for trying. A good baseball player tries his best to get on base, and if he hits .300 he is worth millions, yet he is successful only three out of ten tries." Husbands and wives can think of appropriate things to say when the other partner is experiencing stress. They can help reduce the severity of the stress by sizing up the incident more accurately.

In *It's Not as Tough as You Think* and *It's Not as Tough at Home as You Think*, I cited numerous examples of incidents that were experienced as calamities when they occurred but shrank into insignificance with the passage of time.

Unfortunately, both the husband and wife may react excessively to a stressful incident. However, if either partner can "keep his/her cool," one can defuse what appears to be a major adversity to the other, if only by saying, "Come on, honey. A year from now we'll be laughing about this, so let's start laughing now."

Mood Changes

While roller-coaster mood changes are not normal, neither is it normal to have an unchanging mood throughout one's life. It is understandable that circumstances can affect one's mood. A job promotion or increase in salary gives rise to a cheerful mood, and a notice of a tax audit can result in dejection. A child chosen as valedictorian brings joy, and hearing that a loved one is seriously ill makes one sad. There are a myriad of circumstances that can alter how a person feels. In such cases, we usually know why we feel the way we do, and we can usually adjust to the situation.

However, there are some mood changes that are not easily explained. The colloquialism "I got up on the wrong side of the bed today" indicates that one is dispirited but does not know why. Research has revealed that there are mood changes that may be due to physiological rather than psychological causes.

Emotions are processed by the brain, which is a physical organ just like the heart, lungs and liver. It is obvious that changes in the body chemistry can affect how these organs function. It should come as no surprise that chemical changes in the body can affect the brain and result in emotional changes. It is possible for a person to be dejected even though nothing bad has happened, and it is not because "he got up on the wrong side of the bed," but because there were subtle changes in the body chemistry that altered his mood.

Mild mood changes need not be a reason for concern. If one realizes that one is subject to them, one may say, "Honey, I must be having an off-day today. I don't know why, but it'll pass." It is only when mood changes affect a person's functioning that it may require professional attention.

However, there may be a rather severe mood change which may cause temporary dysfunction, and unless it is identified and managed properly, may result in much misery. While most women have some mild discomfort related to their monthly hormonal cycle, sometimes these changes result in severe symptoms, a condition referred to as PMS, which can be properly treated so that it is not disruptive.

Some symptoms of PMS are irritability, anger, depression, confusion and tension. The woman might flare up at something which she would normally dismiss. She may say harsh words to her husband, parents and in-laws. She may have episodes of unprovoked crying. There may also be physical symptoms, such as water retention, severe headaches, nasal congestion and painful joint swelling. In the classic case, these symptoms may last about a week before culminating in abrupt relief. There are many variations of this pattern.

Irreparable harm may result when a woman who suffers from severe PMS irritability tells her in-laws to "never set foot in this house again." Several days later, when her irritability disappears, she may apologize profusely, but the in-laws may not be very forgiving.

The only way PMS can be diagnosed is by keeping a chart for several months. The woman should note what symptoms she has and mark them on a calendar. If, after several months, the chart shows a relationship of these symptoms to her hormonal cycle, it is very suggestive of PMS.

Understanding, by both husband and wife, that the emotional changes are related to hormonal changes rather than to psychological causes can defuse a potentially volatile situation. There are books available on management of PMS (I also recommend my book, *Getting Up When You're Down*). Many women experience marked alleviation of symptoms by following a PMS diet and taking certain vitamins. Exercise, such as aerobics, swimming, brisk walking or jogging are all helpful. In severe cases, there are some very safe medications that can bring much relief.

Although we are concentrating primarily on the first year, there may be a baby in the first year, and there may be mood changes following the birth. The hormonal changes surrounding pregnancy and delivery may result in a mood change. It is not uncommon for a new mother to have the "baby blues," and although she knows she should feel happy having delivered a healthy baby, she may find herself in tears for no known reason. These "blues" may disappear in a few days.

It is also possible, however, for the depressed mood to persist beyond a few days or for a mother to have frightening feelings. It is important to have an evaluation, because postpartum depressions may be severe. Delaying treatment may result in serious progression of the disease. Whereas rest is important, it may not be enough to dispel the dejected mood. Early treatment of postpartum depression can result in dramatic relief and forestall serious consequences.

*C*harna and Zev were thrilled when she delivered a healthy eight-pound boy. This was Zev's parents first grandchild. They had a gala celebration of both the *bris* and *pidyon haben*. Charna's mother stayed for two weeks, and after she left, Zev was very helpful with the baby. But two months after the delivery, Charna became depressed, frequently crying for no apparent reason. She told Zev that she was not a good wife and he did not deserve to suffer through life with someone like her. She refused to go out or to have friends come over.

Charna's mother came, and concluded that Charna had suffered an *ayin hara* (evil eye) because they had flaunted the gala celebrations. She sought a *tzaddik* who could remove the evil-eye. After several futile attempts, Zev called her doctor, who suggested that Charna was suffering from a postpartum depression. Charna was prescribed medication, and after ten days began to feel better. By the end of a month she was back to her normal self and described the episode as a "nightmare."

Inasmuch as the wife may be expecting in the first year, it is important that both the husband and wife understand the possible discomforts of this situation. Some women are fortunate in not having any difficulty, but there is a spectrum from no symptoms all the way to disabling symptoms. There may be morning sickness which is unpleasant enough, but some women may be nauseous all day and have frequent vomiting. They may react violently to certain odors, such as cigarette smoke, car exhaust fumes or even newsprint.

It is a gross injustice to consider these distressing feelings to be of psychological origin. On a boat trip to Europe, there was a doctor whose seasickness had him leaning over the ship's railing. My mother could not restrain herself from saying, "You doctors say that our nausea is 'all in our minds.' Now you know how we feel, and that it is not all in our minds."

These symptoms generally abate after the first trimester, but sometimes continue much longer. As long as they persist, it is imperative that the husband be very patient, considerate and accommodating. This may be the most difficult days of a woman's life, and the husband should do everything he can to help his wife cope with this discomfort.

Although the wife is the one experiencing the discomfort, we should be aware that the husband, too, experiences some distress. He had married a vivacious, cheerful young woman, who is now feeling very miserable, and although they are both thrilled about having a baby, he may nevertheless feel guilty. He wishes he could help her feel better, but is powerless.

Once the baby is born and the mazal-tov wishes have subsided, the husband has a role in sharing the care of the baby. If the baby is bottle-fed, he may get up to provide the feeding, burping and diapering in the middle of the night. Even if the mother is nursing the baby, he may take the baby from the crib, diaper it, give it to the mother and burp it after the feeding. The husband may claim that he needs his sleep in order to be able to function at the yeshivah or the office the next day. I understand, Dad, but the pregnancy and delivery may have exhausted your wife, and she needs all the rest she can get. Be considerate.

Most fathers are ecstatically happy with the birth of their first child, but it is not unheard of for a new father to actually be a bit resentful that the wife cannot give him her undivided attention any more. In addition, the household no longer runs as efficiently. Tending to the baby, as well as sleep interruption, may leave the wife exhausted. The husband may have to help with the housekeeping. This is an adjustment the husband must make. Parenthood does not come easily to either father or mother.

Both must make sacrifices for the welfare of the child and for the well-being of their marriage.

Becoming parents is a new phase in life, and inasmuch as one has never before had this experience, one must adjust to a number of stresses that this phase introduces. The baby interrupts one's sleep, may be colicky and cry more than anticipated, or may develop a fever or cold symptoms. When you hold the baby and it hiccups, you feel the whole tiny body shake, and the persistent hiccuping may seem endless. Relax. It eventually stops.

There are books on infant care that tell you what you can expect and how to handle the various situations of infancy. You will find reassurance, guidance on what to do and under what circumstances to consult your pediatrician. You will be able to cope efficiently with the problems of infancy, without being anxious.

Having mentioned anxiety, I wish to point out that sometimes the couple may not be expecting in the first two years, and couples who are very desirous of having a baby may become concerned about this, particularly if their friends did have children early in marriage. It has been demonstrated that anxiety may actually be an obstacle to conceiving. Couples should not panic if it does not occur as soon as they had hoped. It is important to be relaxed and confident that you will conceive in due time. Be attuned to your spouse's feelings and bolster each other's confidence. After two years have elapsed, it is wise to consult a specialist in this field.

The Magic Phrases

*T*here are several themes that are recurrent in our prayers. We praise G-d, we declare our love for Him, we express our gratitude to Him, and we admit our wrongdoings and ask for His forgiveness.

Our *sefarim* ask, inasmuch as G-d knows all our thoughts, why must we verbalize our prayers? Is it not enough that we love and praise G-d in our hearts, feel thankful and regret our mistakes? G-d knows our feelings. Why must we express them verbally?

Perhaps, verbalizing our feelings has a secondary benefit. It makes us feel more comfortable when saying these words to other people.

It is not uncommon for children to be reluctant to say "thank you." A mother may tell her 5-year-old child, "Say 'thank you' to the nice man for the candy," and the child only turns away with a grunt. It is even more difficult to get a child to say "I'm sorry." A parent may say, "You should never hit your sister. Now go and apologize to her." Notoriously, the child may resist this as if it were the hardest thing in the world. These traits often persist far into adulthood.

How many marriages might have been saved if only the couple had praised each other more often and had exchanged the three short phrases, "I thank you," "I love you," and "I'm sorry, but I was wrong," more often.

To overcome this resistance, we use these expressions frequently in our prayers, so that we become familiar with the words. If we give some thought to what we are saying to G-d, it may facilitate our saying it to our spouses. How paradoxical it is for a man to return home from shul and make a negative remark to his wife. This is an indication that he did not absorb much from his prayers. Just as loving G-d and praising Him go together, so should love and praise in marriage go together.

A woman told a psychologist, "My child misbehaves mostly at home. Away from home he behaves much better." The psychologist responded, "Madam, don't you?"

Our *mussar* works greatly emphasize *hakaras hatov*, acknowledging the good we have received. They cite the Talmud's teaching that Adam aggravated his sin by blaming Eve, saying to G-d, "The woman that You gave me made me eat it," thereby denying his gratitude to G-d for having given him a wife. Away from home, we are usually careful to say "thank you" when someone does something nice for us. Husbands and wives would do well to say "thank you" to each other for even the little things they do for each other.

I suspect that the difficulty we have with verbalizing these phrases is due to the nemesis I have described in my other books: *poor self-esteem*. Acknowledging a favor may feel demeaning to a person who has a poor self-concept, because it may make him feel that he is beholden to others. Similarly, one may see an expression of love as a sign of dependence on another, which may be very threatening to a person with a low self-concept. Praising others might be seen as meaning that others are better than oneself. Indeed, people who belittle others may be doing so to feel that they are superior to others. And of course, admitting one was wrong is most difficult for someone who already feels he is inadequate.

Historically in Judaism, the husband supported the family and the wife was the homemaker. The woman was the wife and mother, and as Solomon says, "Her children arise and praise her; her husband, and he lauds her" (*Proverbs* 31:28). She felt fulfilled in her role which she saw as dignified and this was a component of self-esteem.

In modern society, the prestige of the woman as mother and homemaker has unfortunately been eroded. Many women consider this role a "second best," and glorify being in the professions or in an important position in commerce. Although the Torah-observant woman knows her priorities, and although economic demands may make it necessary for her to work, she knows that her role as a wife and mother comes first. Yet, there may still be a subconscious nagging envy of the "liberated" woman. The zeal of some extreme feminists may have trivialized homemaking and motherhood and affected the pride of the woman who chooses a primary role as wife and mother.

It is important that the husband be sensitive to this. The Talmud assigns the fortune of the household as being due to the merits of the wife rather than the husband (*Bava Metzia* 59a). Let us remember the words of Solomon, "Hear, my son, *mussar avicha* (discipline of your father), and do not forsake *toras emecha* (the teaching of your mother)" *(Proverbs* 1:8). Solomon chose his words carefully, assigning *mussar* to the father and *Torah* to the mother. It is the mother's love and respect for Torah that stimulates the child's desire to become a Torah scholar. The husband's esteem of the wife can counteract the alien influences of modern society.

"Women are good mothers only if they value their womanhood—their creativity, inner divinity and ability to impact the world, independently of being wives and mothers. Part of a husband's role is to value, nurture and validate this part of his wife's identity" (*Guide for the Romantically Perplexed*, L. Aiken, Devorah Publishers, p. 204).

Some men may have the idea that women were placed in the world to take care of them. We must understand that both men and women were placed in this world to do the will of G-d, and each fulfills his or her mission by doing the will of G-d. The wife's fulfillment of her mission is every bit as worthy as the husband's. This should be expressed both in word and deed.

We have already noted that the Torah frees a man of all external responsibilities, military and civil, during the first year of marriage, so that he may "gladden his wife" (*Deuteronomy* 24:5). Furthermore, Rambam states that at any time during the marriage, a man may not take a job at some distance from the home if this will detract from the relationship with his wife, unless she approves of it (*Hilchos Ishus* 14:2).

There are some generalities that are gender specific. For example, women may have a greater need for intimacy than men, and may want their husbands to spend more time with them. Men, as a rule, may be more assertive in seeking independence and individualism. A wife may feel neglected if the husband has other activities and does not spend as much time with her as she would like. This is a misinterpretation. A man may love his wife dearly, yet have a need to have his own space.

Spouses should relate to each other in a way that will elevate self-esteem. It is understandable that a husband and wife may not agree on everything, but disagreement can be expressed respectfully. In particular, *never* should one spouse criticize the other in the presence of the children.

Rabbi Zelig Pliskin relates that a husband and wife agreed that instead of arguing about who was at fault for whatever went wrong, they would blame it on the *yetzer hara*. "Let's focus our anger and hate on the *yetzer hara* and reserve our love for each other" (*Marriage* p. 307).

This is more than anecdotal. The Talmud relates that there was a couple who got into an argument every week, right before Shabbos. (This is a high risk time for irritability, because so often one realizes at the last moment that something important was forgotten and it may be too late to remedy the situation.) R' Meir stayed with this couple three Friday afternoons until he brought them around to a peaceful relationship. He then heard Satan say, "Woe is to me! R' Meir evicted me from this house" (*Gittin* 52a).

It is important to keep this in mind. Satan seeks to undermine *shalom bayis*, and he is very cunning. He may engineer things so that a couple begins to argue. When a spouse thinks that the partner is at fault about something, it may be Satan that is putting this idea into his/her head. Just as we do not yield to Satan's machinations when he tempts us to eat *tereifah* or violate Shabbos, we should not listen to him when he tries to cause an altercation between husband and wife. You may feel that your grounds for blaming or disagreeing are valid, whereas it is actually the wile of Satan at work.

Let me convey some words of wisdom from my late uncle, the Bobover Rebbe. He suggested, "If your wife did something that offended you, go buy her a gift. Why? Because you should forgive her, but saying that you forgive her may not be enough. *Show* her that you care for her even though she made a mistake. Your action will have a greater impact, and when she feels you are considerate of her, she will be careful not to hurt you."

Advocates of "behavior modification" may disagree with this, saying that one should not reward improper behavior. However, I think the Rebbe was right for yet another reason.

My father would cite the verse of the Friday night *zemiros, Kol mekadesh,* which reads, "Extend Your kindness to those who know You, O jealous and vengeful G-d." He asked, "Would it not have been more appropriate when praying 'Extend Your kindness' to say 'kind and merciful G-d' rather than 'jealous and vengeful G-d'?"

My father answered with the parable about a man who was arrested for throwing a rock at the king. The king did not allow him to be punished, and instead gave him a well-paying position in the palace. The man was remorseful. "How could I have thrown a rock at such a benevolent king?" The king then promoted him, which intensified his remorse.

My father pointed out that one can "punish" with kindness, and that the remorse for doing a wrong can be greater than when the punishment is painful. Therefore, the verse in the *zemiros* means, "O, G-d, if You are going to be jealous and vengeful and punish me for my sins, do it with kindness."

Responding to an offense by attacking the other person is apt to reinforce the offender's behavior as he becomes defensive about his actions. Kindness is a better weapon.

Husbands and wives may have many unmet emotional needs, and it is unrealistic to expect the spouse to provide for all of them. If they feel discontented, they may blame the spouse for their unhappiness. Everyone comes into a marriage with emotional baggage, and spouses should realize that their discontent may stem from within themselves, and is not due to the shortcomings of the partner. *

Having a healthy self-esteem is essential in all relationships, and is especially important in marriage and parenting. In *Ten Steps to Being Your Best* I have provided some suggestions for improving self-esteem. The effort involved in doing this will be well rewarded.

---

* I think it is important to let a spouse know what kinds of things please you. I say this because I heard my mother say, "After fifty years of living with him, I still don't know what foods he enjoys."

I believe that my father did have favorite foods, but felt that if my mother knew this, she would make extra effort to provide them for him. Because he did not wish to impose on her in any way, he did not reveal his preferences.

Although I can commend him for his consideration, I think it was offset by depriving my mother of a way to give him greater pleasure. While spouses should not be demanding, neither should they deprive the partner of a means to please them.

Spouses can help their partners elevate their self-esteem. Be on the alert for opportunities to give positive strokes. "Your idea was great!" "I'm proud of the way you handled that." "Thanks for pointing that out to me." "Your speech was great." "That casserole was really delicious."

There is no dearth of positive strokes if we look for them. Unfortunately, from grade school on we have been conditioned to look for faults rather than for virtues. When your teacher returned your homework or test paper, the red marks pointed out the mistakes. True, sometimes she wrote in the margin, "Good point!," but most often it was the wrong answers that were highlighted rather than the right ones. That's the way society operates. The police officer does not put a commendation on your windshield for having put money in the meter, and so it goes. We should change that approach in the family, and although we may have to point out errors, we should try to highlight the good and proper, sometimes even the good intention in an error.

*F*riday morning, Nechama kneaded the dough, let it rise, then braided the *challos*, intending to bake them when she returned from shopping. Nechama was delayed, and Zalman, who was home nursing a cold, thought he would help by putting them into the oven after they had risen adequately. Not being too familiar with the oven control, he set the control to "broil" instead of "bake." When Nechama returned, she was initially pleased by the aroma, then horrified to see the black crust on the *challos*. Realizing that Zalman had intended to help, she said, "It was thoughtful of you to put the *challos* in the oven for me, but look, dear. This points to 'bake,' and this points to 'broil.' Next time, be sure that it is on 'bake.'"

Another incident. My desk looks like it was hit by a tornado, but I know exactly where everything is. When I returned from vacation, my desk was neat, with all the papers in tidy piles, but I did not have a clue as to where anything was. I said to my secretary, "I really appreciate your effort to clean up my mess, but next time, let's do it together."

There are often silver linings that can be pointed out. You just have to avoid being consumed by anger over the error in order to discover the silver lining.

I had a Talmud teacher who would actually give a boost to our self-esteem when we presented an incorrect argument. He would say (in his inimitable Eastern-European English), "You von hundered puhcent right. Now I going to show you vere you wrong."

We loved to be corrected by him.

With a bit of ingenuity and effort, we can help a spouse feel better about himself or herself. It does wonders for the marriage.

There is a powerful ingredient for *shalom bayis*, and that is for the husband and wife to spend some time learning *mussar* together. *During the first year of marriage, you have a golden opportunity to do this.* Later on, the care of the children may not give you much free time. Study *Pirkei Avos* (*Ethics of the Fathers*) and *Mesillas Yesharim* (*Path of the Just*) or other *mussar* works, if only 20 minutes a day. Discussing the principles of *mussar* together can help you relate to each other in a most caring and sensitive way.

Ezer Kenegdo

*I*n the previous chapter I alluded to an emotional gender difference between men and women. This warrants some elaboration.

The Torah says that G-d said, "It is not good that man be alone; I will make for him a helper corresponding to him" (*Genesis* 2:18). A more literal translation is "a helper *opposite* him."

It is clear from the Torah that a wife is intended to be a *companion* to the husband. She is indeed to be "corresponding" to him, but such correspondence does not mean "similar." To the contrary, the Torah chose the word *kenegdo*, "opposite him," because the correspondence that provides for true companionship requires that husband and wife have different and perhaps even somewhat opposite personality makeups. A relationship between two identical personality types would probably be terribly boring, and hardly an enjoyable companionship.

Allow me to share an amusing story with you.

A young man asked a *shadchan* to find him a wife who is known to be an impossible person to live with. She must be a person who constantly complains, finds fault with everyone and is liberal with negative statements. He said that he had read that if a person suffers torment from a mean wife, he will be spared Gehinnom (purgatory) and go directly to Gan Eden.

After they were married, the wife said, "I know why you married me. You think that I will treat you in a manner that will save you from Gehinnom. No way! You are not going to get into Gan Eden because of me," and she proceeded to relate to him with much love and consideration.

Many young men and women know little of the traits of the other gender. Even though they were exposed to a father, mother, brother or sister, these relationships did not require the understanding of the other gender as is required in marriage. Consequently, they may be caught unawares.

And so, my dear newlyweds, the first thing you should know is that your partner is quite different than you, and that this is precisely what G-d intended. If you are patient, considerate and tolerant, you will discover how these differences can make the *kenegdo* the substrate of a wonderful companionship. If you are impatient, inconsiderate and intolerant, the *kenegdo* can become adversarial. The Talmud says this in so many words; "If one merits, the spouse becomes a helper, if one does not merit, the spouse becomes an adversary" (*Yevamos* 63a).

Give yourself time to learn about each other. Do not be judgmental. Do not jump to conclusions.

When we forfeited our idyllic life in Gan Eden, G-d said to Eve that "your craving shall be for your husband," but to Adam He said, "By the sweat of your brow shall you eat bread" (*Genesis* 2:16-19). The die was cast. The woman's need is primarily for a relationship with the husband, whereas the husband's primary need is to work toward a goal. The goal can be reached only by "the sweat of your brow," i.e., with great effort. The "bread" for which he works may refer to Torah study (*Proverbs* 9:5), which can be acquired only with great effort, or to earning one's livelihood.

In my work with alcoholics I found that very often a wife's threat that she would leave if the husband did not stop drinking was ineffective. In fact, even if the wife left with the children, that still may not have brought the husband around. However, the employer's threat to fire him frequently resulted in his prompt application for treatment. I am convinced that this was not because the man did not love his wife and children. Rather, it is a question of *identity*. Men generally define themselves as workers and breadwinners. To lose this is tantamount to losing his very identity, and a man may perceive his loss of job as if he were passing out of existence. Men generally like to be respected for their achievements, and although they may love the wife and children intensely, this need to be respected may actually be more vital to them than the love of the family.

Unless you appreciate the gender differences, you might be flabbergasted when you go on a weekend trip. It took you 15 minutes to put everything you need into a one-suiter, whereas it took your wife more than 3 hours to fill two huge suitcases. "We're only going for two days," you say, "not for two weeks!" At home you have three pairs of shoes, while she just bought her eighteenth pair. Relax. You are normal, so is she.

As a rule, men tend to be a bit more pragmatic and goal-oriented. "Of what use is this" is more likely a man's attitude, whereas the woman may enjoy the feeling of the present and not focus on whether or not there is a defined goal.

It has been quipped that what women want is to be loved, to be listened to, to be desired, to be respected, to be needed and to be trusted. What men in the secular world want is tickets to the Super-Bowl. Although this is not quite accurate, it does say something about the gender difference. Men, too, wish to be loved, to be listened to, to be desired, to be respected, to be needed and to be trusted. They are just not as likely to admit it, even to themselves, because they may interpret any emotional neediness as a sign of weakness.

As is evident from the verse of Torah cited on the previous page, the woman's greatest need is for a relationship. Rashi says that companionship is a woman's priority *(Kiddushin* 7a). From my work, I infer that women more often wish to preserve a problematic marriage than men. Wives will generally stay with an alcoholic husband longer than a husband will stay with an alcoholic wife.

We can see where the husband's need for individuality, independence and autonomy may conflict with the wife's need for being, as the Torah says, "one flesh." It is, therefore, possible that a husband may see his wife's desire for "oneness" as a threat to his individuality. Unless this is properly understood and appropriately accommodated, it may develop into a rather serious problem. If the husband feels his wife's need for oneness is a threat to his individuality, he may defensively pull away from her. This may increase her desire for closeness, which in turn can result in his further withdrawal, and this may spiral out of control.

On the other hand, if the wife understands that the husband's need for individuality is not an indication of his lack of love for her, and the husband understands that his wife's need for companionship is not a threat to his independence, the mutual respect for each others' needs can allow for a reasonable and satisfactory fulfillment of both.

This is predicated on both partners having essentially normal needs. When needs become excessive, professional help may be necessary to preserve a relationship. In cases where the needs of both partners are excessive, chronic discontent may result. It has been said that "If I am attached to another person because I cannot stand on my own two feet, he or she may be a lifesaver, but the relationship can hardly be one of true love."

I saw David and Beverly separately in therapy. (This was in my early days as a psychiatrist when I did not understand that this was unwise.) David had been orphaned at an early age and was raised in an orphanage, where his needs for maternal nurturing were completely frustrated. He married Beverly, who was raised in an abusive home and was starved for love. Each had such inordinate needs to *receive* love that they could not *provide* love for the other. They were both obese, having turned to food for emotional gratification. They were chronically at odds with each other because their dependency needs were insatiable.

Gender differences are generalizations, and there are certainly many exceptions. Nevertheless, appreciating these generalizations may prevent misunderstandings.

The jokes about men driving 20 miles in the wrong direction because they refused to ask for directions have a basis in reality. As a rule, men take pride in demonstrating their competence and self-sufficiency.

Men may feel that being masculine means that one should be macho and stoic, and consequently "men don't cry." As a result, instead of feeling hurt and crying, they are likely to express anger. Women, on the other hand, may feel that to be enraged is not ladylike, hence when they feel angry, they cry as if they were hurt, which is more acceptable to them.

So keep in mind that men's anger may mean that they feel hurt, and women's crying may mean that they feel angry. The masculine concept of stoicism may cause men to deny many feelings.

According to the Talmud, women are more loquacious than men (*Kiddushin* 49b). There are also gender differences in the type of talk. Men tend to be more concrete and offer advice and solutions to problems. Women tend to talk for emotional bonding.

There is a cartoon strip where the wife calls the husband that her car broke down and could he please come and help her. A few moments later, the husband calls, "There's a tow-truck on the way." The wife remarks, "I'm looking for sympathy, and he's giving me solutions."

When women present problems, they want to be understood and share their feelings, whereas men want to suggest how to solve problems. This may cause a communication problem, if, instead of empathizing with his wife, the husband suggests a solution. The wife may become upset that her feelings were not appreciated.

Saying the right thing may alleviate a situation instead of inflaming it.

WRONG:

WIFE: It was so frustrating today. I had plenty of time after my dentist's appointment to pick up the kids from school, but there was a tractor-trailer jackknifed on the highway and I was stuck for over half an hour. I couldn't call anyone to pick them up, and I knew they'd be standing out there waiting for me, which they were.

HUSBAND: I've told you not to leave the house without the cell phone just because of unexpected things like that.

How is this reprimand going to help things? An appropriate comment at a later time when the wife leaves the house would be, "Don't forget the cell phone, Honey." Criticizing her, especially when she has been upset at being so late, can only make her feel worse.

RIGHT:

WIFE: It was so frustrating today. I had plenty of time after my dentist's appointment to pick up the kids from school, but there was a tractor-trailer jackknifed on the highway and I was stuck for over half an hour. I couldn't call anyone to pick them up, and I knew they'd be standing out there waiting for me, which they were.

| **HUSBAND:** | I know how irritating that can be. I once missed a plane because of a traffic obstruction. You're stuck when you can't even get off the highway to take an alternate route. |
| **WIFE:** | What was worse was that I didn't have the cell phone with me to call someone to pick them up. I'm going to have to make sure that I take the phone with me whenever I leave the house. |

The husband was empathic, identifying with her feeling. The wife came to the conclusion of always taking the cell phone with her, without being put down as inept. Of course, the reverse may also be true. A man complaining about his irascible boss does not need to be told to look for another job. He knows that solution. He wants his wife to recognize that he is frustrated at work.

It is always important to validate others' feelings. We are responsible for our actions. We cannot always control our feelings. If someone insults us, we feel angry, and saying "You should not feel angry" is both pointless and irritating.

As an intern, I helped subdue a patient who had gone wild because of insulin shock. Because his brain was without sugar, he was fighting us off and was completely unaware of what he was doing. I succeeded in getting an injection of glucose into him, but not before he had landed a solid blow to my jaw. Once the glucose was injected, he immediately came to, and seeing all the people around, he said, "Did anything happen here?" He had no recollection of what had happened, and certainly had not intended to hit me. However, my jaw hurt badly, and it was he who had done it. My intellect told me there was no reason for me to be angry at him, but there is part of my psyche that is not ruled by intellect. I could not help feeling angry.

Whether a person's feelings are justified or not, they do exist. An appropriate comment is, "I can understand that you feel: angry, hurt, envious, embarrassed, exploited, etc." That is validating the feeling. You may later say, "If you think it over, you will see that there is no reason to *remain*: angry, hurt, envious, embarrassed, exploited, etc."

Men may prefer silence, and women may misinterpret this silence as withdrawal. Husbands should provide a listening ear and realize that keeping silent can be very frustrating. They should empathize with the wife and show their empathy by asking pertinent questions.

Two people can look at the same thing and see it differently. *Empathy* means seeing things through the other person's eyes, and trying to understand their point of view. Inasmuch as we generally assume that our perceptions are correct, we may not realize that other people's perceptions may be different. Empathizing with a spouse is a willingness to understand how he/she sees and understands things.

The Vilna Gaon stressed the importance of empathy. "When talking to someone who thinks differently than you, *especially when that person is being irrational* (italics mine), enter the other person's world and answer him according to his line of reasoning. It is important to remember not to reply according to your own logic, but in a way consistent with his distorted way of thinking in order to ensure that your communication will be accepted" (*Beur HaGra, Proverbs* 26:5). This is an invaluable psychological insight.

I italicized "*especially when that person is being irrational*" because what we think to be an irrational statement may unfortunately sometimes elicit the response, "You don't know what you're talking about," or even "You're crazy." These are insulting and demeaning words which have no place whatever in a couple's communication.

As a resident in psychiatric training, I told my supervisor that my patient's attitude was totally unrealistic. My supervisor said, "Twerski, you're talking logic. She's talking emotion." According to her emotional perception, she was being very realistic. It is important to remember that logic and emotion do not follow the same rules. If something sounds irrational, a proper response is, "I didn't see it that way. Can you help me understand why you think this is so."

A man once complained to a wise man that he was having problems at home. "Go home and listen to what your wife says, and come back in a week." When the man returned, the wise man said, "Now go back and listen to what she *doesn't* say."

Women, more than men, may say things in a way that has more than the literal meaning. After picking up her husband from work, she may say, "Would you want to stop off somewhere for a bite?" If the husband responds, "No, I'd just as soon eat at home. We've got a lot of leftovers in the refrigerator," he has not heard her. Think for a moment. The wife knows very well what's in the refrigerator. Her question was really a statement, "*I'd* like to stop off for a bite." As the wise man said, it is important to hear what she does *not* say.

The popular idea that women are more intuitive than men has a basis in Talmud: "G-d gave women more *binah* than men" (*Niddah* 48b), and *binah* is the capacity to make inferences (*Sanhedrin* 93b). Women can sense things more than men. This does not mean that all of a woman's ideas must be accepted, but they should be given serious consideration. It is not unusual for a man to realize that something he has just discovered had been known to his wife much earlier.

It is important that husbands be aware that the job of a homemaker is *real work*, every bit as taxing and demanding as what they do at their job, and sometimes even more so. On the verse in *Exodus* (1:13), "The Egyptians enslaved the Children of Israel with crushing hardness," the Talmud comments that they gave the men's work to the women and the women's work to the men (*Tanchuma, Vayeitzei* 9). Inasmuch as the men's work was making bricks and carrying heavy loads, it is easily understandable why this was "crushing hardness" for women. But why was women's work "crushing hardness" for men? Obviously, the Talmud is telling us that women's work is anything but easy.

When the husband comes home from the yeshivah, office or plant tired and exhausted, he should understand that the wife may be just as tired and exhausted as he is, and she may be in need of a period of rest no less than he is.

Secrets are often the ruination of a marriage. I am often asked whether a prospective *chassan* or *kallah* should reveal health problems before engagement. If the problem is such that it could affect the marriage in any way, it must be revealed. Discovery that significant information was withheld undermines trust, and trust is the cement that binds a couple.

Several months after their marriage, when Esther was already expecting their first child, she happened to discover some pills in Efraim's *tallis* bag. He told her these were vitamins, but Esther was suspicious. Why would he hide vitamins in his tallis bag? She took the pills to the pharmacist, who identified them as medication used for treatment of a psychiatric condition. Confronted with this, Efraim admitted that at age 18 he developed a depressive condition, and was told to take this medication indefinitely.

"Why didn't you tell me about this before we were engaged?" Esther asked.

"My father instructed me not to tell. I was obeying my father's order," Efraim said.

Esther called her father, who had became furious and called Efraim's father, giving him a dressing down and insisting on an immediate divorce, the baby notwithstanding. Efraim's father claimed he had asked a *gadol* (halachic authority), who had told him that it was not necessary to reveal this information, but he refused to say who this *gadol* was.

Esther was not interested in a divorce. She said that she loved Efraim and did not blame him, because he had to obey his father. However, she felt that his father was dishonest and deceptive, and she wanted nothing to do with her in-laws. Efraim agreed that his father had given him bad advice. Esther had a beautiful baby, and she and Efraim get along well. However, she refuses to let the in-laws see their grandchild. Efraim's father tried to apologize, but Esther would not even accept his calls.

Had Esther not justified Efraim's withholding the information, the marriage would have been terminated. Information that the other spouse has a right to know because it could affect him/her should not be kept secret. [Incidentally, the presence of a depression does increase the incidence in the offspring slightly.]

However, in this case, where the first episode was in adolescence, there is great likelihood of recurrence. Couples can weather this, but when it is hidden there is resentment at being deceived. According to halachah there may be grounds for a mandatory *get* as this was a concealed blemish and therefore the marriage was agreed to on fraudulent terms.

However, husbands and wives should understand that if something was told to them in confidence, they may not reveal it to each other. The prohibition against *lashon hara* (defamatory speech) and *rechilus* (carrying tales) applies to husbands and wives as well as to friends and strangers.

Sometimes a spouse will refrain from sharing information in order to protect the partner from pain, such as not revealing to him that someone he/she cared for was in a serious accident or had died. Whether to reveal this or not is a matter of personal judgment, and if the spouse later says, "Why didn't you tell me?" he/she will be appreciative of the partner's concern even though he/she may wish they had known.

*T*he sister of HaGaon R' Shlomo Zalman Auerbach asked him about a student in his yeshivah who was suggested as a *shidduch* for her

daughter. R' Shlomo Zalman said, "He is a very fine young man."
When his sister was leaving, she told R' Shlomo Zalman that she
was going to visit their sister who lived in the neighborhood.

When the sister emerged from the other sibling's house after
the visit, she found R' Shlomo Zalman outside, patiently waiting for
her. He said, "That young man that you mentioned, he is indeed a
fine young man, but he is not appropriate for your daughter."

"But why did you have to wait out here to tell me that?"
the sister asked. "You could have told me that when I was at
your house."

"I couldn't," R' Shlomo Zalman said, "because my wife was
present. I had to tell *you*, because it affects the *shidduch* for your
daughter. But inasmuch as it does not affect my wife, my making a negative comment about the young man — which she
would hear — is *lashon hara*."

That is how cautious we must be to avoid *lashon hara*, even between
those as close as husband and wife.

Decisions, Decisions

*W*e make countless decisions every day. We generally do not think of many things we do as results of decisions, but which suit or dress to wear is a decision, as is what to cook for dinner or whether to go by car or public transportation. However, there are decisions that are much more significant, which can affect others as well as ourselves.

Decision-making should be a joint venture. There may be areas in which either spouse may sign off. For example, the husband may not have an opinion on what kind of drapes to get for the living room, and the wife may not have an opinion on who should be the family's halachic authority. However, on issues on which both spouses do have an opinion, decisions should be reached after discussion. Although there may be differences, each spouse should respect the other's opinion.

When making decisions, whether in unanimity or otherwise, several points should be borne in mind.

- Do we have all the facts? Sometimes decisions are based on hearsay or fragmentary information. Knee-jerk decisions are often made without knowledge of all the facts, and such decisions are frequently regretted.

- How will this decision affect others? We should consider how a decision may affect other family members, neighbors and friends. If a decision which may be advantageous to us will cause ill-feeling to others, the negatives may outweigh the positives. This does not mean that we may not exercise our rights, but rather that we should consider the possible consequences.

- Have we investigated all options? Sometimes the optimum decision is overlooked because one has simply not considered viable alternatives.

- Is this an emotionally charged issue? If so, we are apt to be biased, and our perception of both facts and options may be grossly distorted.

Wherever possible, let every decision be tentative and open for reconsideration. Sometimes we may be obstinate, seeing a change of mind as being indecisive. Being inflexible is as bad as flip-flopping. Rethinking a decision is often wise.

In considering several options, try to imagine yourself living with each option. How does this make you feel? Are you happier with one option than with another? Adding a room for the new arrival may certainly have advantages, but it will result in a debt burden. Try to think about how you will feel with having a nursery, and will the worry about unpaid bills exceed the convenience and pleasure of a nursery.

If it is not necessary to make an immediate decision, allow yourself to sleep on it. You'll be surprised how a night's rest can clarify the issues.

Finally, don't hesitate to consult an outsider, e.g., parents, extended family, rabbis or professionals. An objective view may be very enlightening.

Fashioning Happiness

*C*an happiness be fashioned? Isn't happiness often due to circumstances?

Listen to what the Talmud says: "When our love was strong, we could lie on the thin edge of a sword, but now, a 60-cubit bed is not big enough for us" (*Sanhedrin* 7a). Circumstances do not create nor ruin happiness.

Early in his marriage, Dr. Les Parrott was frustrated because he and his wife were having it so much more difficult than some other couples. He relates an incident which was enlightening to him and an insight which should be equally illuminating for everyone:

> A truth hit me in the most unlikely of all places: a statistics course. In the midst of learning about cybernetics and multiple regressions, I sat down at the console of a computer and began to enter data. After 45 minutes, I finally got all the

lines and columns in their proper places. I hit the panel with the palm of my hand and sat back in the swivel chair to watch it perform. But nothing happened. There was total and absolute silence. I was just getting ready to kick the machine when I looked up above regular eye-level to a white panel that was now illuminated. And there in simple numbers and plain English was the answer to my statistical problem.

I could not believe it. I thought the machine would cycle and recycle and flash multicolored lights as it analyzed the variables I had entered. But it had taken the computer only seven-hundredths of a second to give me my results.

I slumped in my chair, feeling inadequate, when my professor, Dr. Wallis, came along. "What's the trouble, Les?" he asked.

I told him how long it took me to put my problem into the computer and how it took only a millisecond for the computer to give me an answer. "How in the world can it do that?" I asked.

Dr. Wallis took my question seriously, telling me how a computer takes one iota of data and gives it a positive electrical impulse and stores it, or gives it a negative electrical impulse and stores it. After that, the computer simply recalls the information from its memory and combines it in new ways. Then he said, "It basically works like a human brain."

"What do you mean?" I asked.

"Our brains are programmed much like a computer. Just before we put any sound, sight, smell, taste, touch or intuition into our mental computers, we stamp it as 'positive' or 'negative.' Then we store the sensation in our brains, and it permanently stays there. That's why you can't always remember a person's name, but you can always remember how you felt about them."

Knowing that I was more interested in psychology than cybernetics, Dr. Wallis added, "Unlike computers, however, *humans develop a habit of programming their minds to be either mostly negative or mostly positive*" (italics mine).

That's when it dawned upon me: I was making myself and our marriage miserable, sitting around waiting for opportunity to come knocking and complaining because it wasn't. Without even knowing it, I had developed a bad habit of stamping my circumstances as "negative." Instead of making the best of our conditions, I was wallowing in self-pity and allowing them to make the best of me.

That afternoon in the computer lab was a turning point for me. From then on, I determined to be happy no matter what. Not that I am always optimistic and on top of the world, *but I now refuse to let my circumstances determine my mood—or my marriage* (italics mine). It all began by my realizing just how destructive a negative attitude is to a person—and a partnership (*Saving Your Marriage Before It Starts*" pp. 56-57).

The Talmud says, "Who is wealthy? One who is happy with his lot" (*Ethics of the Fathers* 4:10). The statement, "I now refuse to let my circumstances determine my mood" is merely a restatement of the Talmudic principle. Granted, this is not an easy attitude to develop, but we should work toward it. Strengthening our *emunah* (faith) can enable us to have a much happier attitude.

There is no denying that circumstances have an impact on one's attitude. There is certainly a difference between being notified that one has won the sweepstake or being notified that one has been in serious tax arrears. However, two people can be affected differently by circumstances, depending on whether their basic attitude is positive or negative, as demonstrated by this story of two children.

One child was taken into a room full of toys. Looking at the carpentry set, he said, "I'll probably puncture my finger and get blood poisoning." Looking at the baseball bat and glove he said, "I'll probably get hit in the head by a line drive." Looking at the bicycle he said, "I'll probably bump into a rock, get thrown off the bike and fracture my skull." A second child was taken into a room full of manure. He clapped his hands in glee. "There must be a pony around here somewhere!" he said.

$\mathcal{E}$ velyn was a very negative person. If Arnold would come home with the cheerful news that he had just closed a deal with a $10,000 profit, Evelyn would say, "My brothers could make a half-million dollar deal, and you would never hear them even mention it." Arnold tried his best to please Evelyn, but she would find a dark side to everything. Needless to say, they had a miserable marriage.

Another factor that can subvert the marriage relationship is the all-too-common tendency to *blame*. This tendency goes back to the origin of mankind. Adam blamed Eve and Eve, in turn, blamed the serpent. No one was forgiven. Had they said, "I did wrong and I regret it," perhaps they might have been forgiven instead of punished. G-d forgives more readily if a person promptly admits his mistake and does *teshuvah*. "For this I shall judge you, for saying 'I did not sin' " (*Jeremiah* 2:35), and "One who confesses and atones shall obtain mercy" (*Proverbs* 28:13). Although Adam did subsequently admit and do *teshuvah*, the punishment had already been declared.

Nothing can ignite and fuel an argument like blaming. Blaming achieves nothing and results in a negative attitude. The destructiveness of blaming is increased exponentially when one says, "You never do anything right."

Blaming can be totally irrational yet make some kind of sense to people who refuse to accept responsibility for their actions. It is not unusual for a wife batterer to say, "Look what you made me do." Most blaming can be avoided if a person will take responsibilities for his/her behavior.

Just how prone we may be to resort to blaming can be seen from the following teaching in the Torah. The matriarch, Rachel, desperately wanted to have children, especially since her sister, Leah, had borne four sons. She cried to Jacob," Give me children—otherwise I am dead" (*Genesis* 30:1). When Rachel finally had a child, she said, "G-d has taken away my disgrace" (ibid. v. 23). What disgrace? Rashi quotes the Midrash which says that in the absence of children, a woman has no one to blame for things that are broken or missing. Now that Rachel had a child, she would have *someone to blame for missing or broken things*.

Pause a moment to think. Is it conceivable that the matriarch Rachel, to whom a childless life was not worth living, could have welcomed the birth of the child for whom she had so yearned with the thought, "Now I will have someone to blame"? This is the height of absurdity. Although this was certainly not the case with Rachel, the Midrash makes this statement to teach us how vulnerable we are to blaming. Knowing our propensity, we should be especially on guard that we do not resort to blaming.

The flip side of blaming is making excuses, in the attempt to exonerate oneself from a mistake. If you really wish to avoid problems, whether in marriage or other relationships, follow the rule cited earlier, "Never defend a mistake." We begin the morning services by saying, "Let a person always be G-d fearing ... and *acknowledge the truth.*" This principle should be followed throughout the day. You may pay a short-term price for acknowledging the truth, but the long-term gain surpasses this by far.

Some people seem to have a Ph.D. in "excusiology." They may outrightly deny making a mistake, blame someone else for it, and if these fail, make excuses. Excuses which are patently ridiculous seem to make good sense to them.

It is unrealistic to see anything in human life as providing uninterrupted bliss, and marriage is no exception. If a couple does not have unrealistic expectations, their marriage can be a happy one, even if there are moments of displeasure and frustration. The Declaration of Independence says that "the pursuit of happiness" is an inalienable human right. True. *Pursuing* happiness is indeed a human right. Everyone may pursue happiness. *Acquiring* happiness, especially what one *may define* as happiness, is not an inalienable human right. Accepting this may prevent much frustration.

Problems in Marital Relations

*O*ut of concern for *tzenius*, printed information about problems in marital relations for a Torah observant couple is scarce. It is precisely the lack of information and often inadequate preparation for marriage that is responsible for many of the problems that occur early in marriage. When identified early and submitted to competent counseling, progression of problems and their impact on the relationship can be avoided.

In his excellent book, *Man and Wife—the Shechinah Abides With Them* (currently available in Hebrew), R' Eliashiv Kenuel has provided a supplement which discusses marital relations from a Torah perspective, and clarifies much of the confusion that prevails. In the Introduction, R' Kenuel writes these important lines:

"It is clearly impossible, however, to relate to every possible problem in so short a booklet. It should be emphasized that nothing forces a couple to live with problems without trying to solve them. Should problems arise, it is recommended that the couple consult a trained marital counselor.

"Before seeking outside assistance, it is important that the couple engage in open and frank discussion. Both partners should remember that the marital bond transformed them into 'one body' (*Genesis* 2:24), so that there is no reason to hide things from each other. Such discussions may not be easy at first, but they owe it to themselves to make the effort. In the absence of a genuine attempt to address the troubling issues and reach understanding and agreement, it will be almost impossible to achieve intimacy that is pleasurable and satisfying."

Adequate understanding of respective roles in intimacy *before* marriage is invaluable in forestalling problems. Men should understand the feminine response and women should understand the masculine response. Ignorance of what is required for emotional bonding is the culprit in many marriage problems.

The profound and sensitive emotions involved in marital relations make them exquisitely vulnerable to the deleterious effects of anxiety. Unless addressed promptly, the anxiety engendered by problems aggravates them, setting into motion a vicious cycle. Given patience and mutual consideration, some problems may resolve themselves without professional attention. However, early consultation with a competent counselor will guide the couple as to whether patience and mutual consideration are sufficient in their case, or whether professional counseling is necessary.

Misunderstandings in this vital area of marriage can have far-reaching consequences. Those who give *chassan* classes and *kallah* classes are generally aware of competent counselors who should be consulted.

A Spiritual Marriage

*D*efining a spiritual marriage requires repetition of some of the components discussed in earlier chapters, but this is justified in order to unite the various segments into a whole.

Spirituality requires effort, much effort. We are born into the world essentially as animal bodies with all the drives characteristic of animals. As we mature, we are supposed to develop ourselves into the dignified human beings G-d intended us to be.

In *Let Us Make Man*, I cited the Baal Shem Tov's interpretation of the verse in *Genesis* (1:6), "And G-d said, 'Let us make man.' " The obvious question is: Whom was G-d addressing? Furthermore, G-d did not seek anyone's involvement in any other part of creation. Why was the creation of man unique in this way?

The Baal Shem Tov explained that both angels and animals are born essentially in a state of completion and do not have to transform themselves. Those creatures that do undergo transformation, such as the tadpole and caterpillar, do so automatically, because the transformation is programmed into their genes. It is not a voluntary decision and effort to change.

Man is uniquely different. Man is born in a *state of potential*, and he must transform himself into being a spiritual being. A person who is completely spiritual upon birth would be just another type of angel. After creating angels, it was G-d's wish to create a being that would work toward becoming spiritual. Hence, G-d needed man's participation in the formation of man. It is for this reason that the Talmud says that a spiritual person "becomes a partner with G–d in the work of creation" (*Shabbos* 119a).

Inasmuch as G-d needed man's participation in becoming the being He intended man to be, G-d's statement, "Let us make man" was addressed to man himself. "You and I together can create man. I will give you the potential, but you must develop it. If I create you fully spiritual, you would be an angel rather than a man."

Transforming ourselves into spiritual beings does not come about easily. Many animalistic drives must be overcome, subdued or sublimated. The animal nature within us that is antithetic to spirituality is never eliminated and to the very last day of our lives seeks to dominate us. The development of spirituality is a constant, ongoing struggle.

"G-d created man in His likeness" (*Genesis* 1:27). The goal of spiritual man is to become "in the likeness of G-d," which the Talmud says means that a person should emulate the Divine attributes. (For elaboration on spirituality, see *Twerski on Spirituality*.) On the verse, "In the likeness of G-d He created him; male and female He created them" (ibid.), R' Samson Raphael Hirsch says that both genders were created in the likeness of G-d.

Although the Torah refers to Eve as being fashioned out of Adam's rib, the Talmud explains that Adam and Eve were created as a single unit, and that the creation of Eve consisted of her being separated from Adam (ibid. *Rashi*). It was this single unit, therefore, that was created in the likeness of G-d. Man without woman is incomplete (*Zohar* 3:81), and cannot achieve the goal of creation. This undoubtedly is the meaning of the statement by R' Elazar, "A person without a wife is not *adam* (man), because the Torah says 'G-d created them male and female and called *their* name *adam*'" (*Yevamos* 63a). True spirituality is achieved when man and woman are united in a spiritual union.

Spirituality is what distinguishes man from lower forms of life. This is why the Talmud says that a *rasha* (wicked person) is considered dead even during his lifetime (*Berachos* 18b). Although a *rasha* is physiologically alive, it is only the animal component within him that is living. Without the unique human quality, spirituality, he is dead *as a person.*

Animals are totally self-centered. With the exception of pets which may acquire certain human behaviors, animals are not altruistic. Animals in the wild do not sacrifice their own desires and comfort for the welfare of other animals. Human beings should be "other-centered." To the degree that one cares for other people, to that degree one is truly human.

A spiritual marriage can only be one in which each partner is motivated in the welfare, well-being and happiness of the other. This is why the Talmud specifies that "a husband should love his wife as himself and should respect her even more than himself" (*Yevamos* 62b). In order to be spiritual, one's concern for the other must exceed one's concern for oneself.

The title of this book indeed emphasizes the importance of the first year as the foundation of an enduring marriage. However, proper launching of the marriage is not enough. The effort to develop a spiritual marriage must be ongoing throughout the marriage.

The Midrash says: "The pairing of a couple is as difficult as the dividing the waters of the Red Sea" (*Vayikra Rabbah* 8:1). R' Kenuel in *Man and Wife—the Shechinah Abides With Them* explains that anyone can divide water just by slicing it with his hand. However, the water does not remain divided, returning immediately to its previous state. The miracle of the Red Sea was that after the water was divided, it *remained* divided. The analogy to marriage is that it is not too difficult for a man and woman to initiate a spiritual relationship. The challenge is *maintaining* a spiritual relationship throughout the marriage. There are countless stresses during the marriage that evoke the animalistic biological response of giving priority to one's own comfort and gratification. Overcoming these and making the partner's needs primary is the mettle of a spiritual marriage.

The only true union is a spiritual union. Physical bodies have boundaries, and there can never be a true fusion. This is why Rashi comments on the verse "and they shall become one flesh" (*Genesis* 2:24), "The child is created through both, and there they become one flesh." Physical unity can occur only in the child. A true bond of husband and wife can be only spiritual.

Our bodies have limitations, our *neshamos* do not. *Neshamos* can fuse; bodies remain distinct. To the degree that one gives emphasis to one's body, to that degree one gives emphasis to that component of our being that separates us. To the degree that one gives emphasis to the *neshamah*, to that degree one gives emphasis to that component of our being that binds us.

One couple consulted me as the "last resort" for saving their marriage. They had done everything right "by the book" to assure that they would have a happy marriage. They had premarital counseling, adjusted faulty expectations, read books, attended seminars and even had counseling on effective communications. They felt that they were very much in love. Yet, in spite of all this, six years into their marriage, they were unhappy. Being unable to find what was wrong, they had come to the conclusion that they were just mismatched.

It was evident that they had not listened to the *berachah* at their wedding, which referred to Jewish marriage as *kiddushin*, holiness. The Talmud says that "man and wife—the *Shechinah* (Divine Presence) abides with them" (*Sotah* 17a), but the *Shechinah* must be made welcome.

When R' Mendel of Kotzk came to his master, R' Bunim of P'shis'che, the latter asked him, "Young man, where can you find G-d?"

R' Mendel replied, "G-d is everywhere. His glory fills the entire universe."

R' Bunim asked again, "Young man, where can you find G-d?"

R' Mendel said, "If my answer is not good, then you tell me."

R' Bunim said, "G-d can be found wherever He is invited and made welcome."

If husband and wife behave in a manner that is politically correct but lacks *kedushah*, their home is not one that welcomes the Divine Presence.

R' Shlomo Zalman Auerbach was accompanied by a student. Before he entered his home, R' Shlomo Zalman paused to brush the dust from his coat. He explained to the student, "The Talmud says that 'man and wife, the *Shechinah* abides with them.' It is disrespectful to be in the presence of the *Shechinah* with a dusty garment."

A true Torah-observant home is certainly most conducive to the Divine Presence. However, we should remember that as important as observance of mitzvos is, it is possible, as Ramban says in *Leviticus* 19:2, for a person to be in technical compliance with every halachic requirement, and nevertheless be a vulgar person. Ramban makes this comment on the verse in the Torah which says, "*kedoshim tihiu,* you shall be holy" The Midrash says (*Vayikra Rabbah* 13:3) that the mitzvos were given to us *for no reason other than to refine our middos* (character traits).

It is important to study the works of *mussar* and read the biographies of our great Torah personalities to learn how the performance of mitzvos can lead to character refinement. It is only then that we can become *kadosh* and that the marriage can indeed be *kiddushin.*

G-d is eternal, and His presence in the marriage can endow it with eternity.

Sharing Responsibilities

*T*he roles of husbands and wives are often decided by the culture. Years ago, the husband was the breadwinner and the wife was the homemaker, or the husband devoted his entire day to Torah study and the wife took care of the store. Even when the wife was the one who supported the family, she also functioned as the homemaker. Husbands generally did not feel that they had to share the responsibility of homemaking. That was a woman's assignment.

I believe that the Torah attitude is shown by two anecdotes involving the Steipler Gaon:

A kollel young man consulted the Steipler for guidance in methodology of Torah study. Having received the Steipler's advice, the young man was about to leave, when the Steipler called him back.

"I see that you are a *masmid* (diligent scholar)," the Steipler said. "You must also remember to help your wife with the house-work."

The young man responded, "It is my wife's fervent wish that I spend all my time learning Torah."

"That is *her* mitzvah," the Steipler said. "*Your* mitzvah is to help with the housework."

※ ※

*O*n another occasion, the Steipler asked a young man whether he helped his wife prepare for Shabbos. "Of course," the young man said. "The *Shulchan Aruch* says that the *Amoraim* (Talmudic sages) did something in preparation for Shabbos. I always do something."

The Steipler said, "That is not what I mean. The 'something' that you do is for the mitzvah of *kevod Shabbos* (honoring Shabbos). I am talking about helping your wife, such as doing the *sponga* (washing the floor). That is a mitzvah of its own."

I am not sure what mitzvah the Steipler was referring to, but inasmuch as helping with the housework can enhance *shalom bayis*, it is certainly part of that mitzvah. Or, perhaps it falls under the rubric of *nosei b'ol im chaveiro* (sharing the burden of another person), which the Talmud considers an essential prerequisite for acquisition of Torah (*Ethics of the Fathers* 6:6).

Some husbands may feel that helping with the housework is beneath their dignity. I can personally testify that I saw *gedolim* washing dishes and doing *sponga*.

Husbands and wives who ask one another, "What can I do to help?" are likely to have a happy marriage.

Raising Children

Yes, I know. You've been married only for a short while, and if you do have a child before the end of the first year, there will certainly not be an immediate need to do any child rearing with a tiny infant.

However, when the child does become old enough to be the recipient of child-raising principles, parents may not have thought of a unified approach to child rearing, There is generally very little attention paid to parenting techniques in advance. Unfortunately, parents may not become interested in parenting techniques until the child presents some kind of behavior problem. The adage about an ounce of prevention being better than a pound (*or ton*) of cure is certainly applicable here. Good parenting can forestall many problems.

But what constitutes good parenting? Most people probably raise their children the way they were raised, and parenting techniques have probably been handed down this way from generation to generation since Adam and Eve. However, in today's generation, this is not good enough.

First, not everyone is really delighted with the way they were raised. They may look back and wish that things had been handled differently. But even assuming that you were fortunate in being the beneficiary of excellent parenting, your spouse may also feel that way about herself/himself. Yet, you may have both received very different types of parenting. If your spouse's inherited method of parenting is different than yours, your children will be subjected to two diverse parenting concepts, which can be very confusing and leave a child without clear direction. *There is nothing as detrimental to child rearing as a lack of a congruent approach by both parents.* The Talmud says that a *ben sorer u'moreh* (a rebellious and defiant son) is not condemned if his parents did not speak with one voice (*Sanhedrin* 71a). He cannot be held fully responsible for defying his parents if they were even minimally divergent in their discipline.

But let me take it a step further. Even if both parents inherited similar parenting techniques, they would still fall short of meeting today's needs. Society is changing at an unprecedented rate. Some norms and values that were accepted just several years ago have been discarded. The moral decadence that prevails in modern society is alarming. We may do our utmost to protect our families from the harmful influences of the environment, but there is no foolproof insulation. Parenting today is a much greater challenge than ever before in history.

So, during this first year, avail yourselves of material on parenting and discuss it. There are different schools of thought on approaches to good parenting, and each author advocates his particular method as being most effective. The particular method you choose is not critical. What is important is that you both use the same method. Naturally, I would recommend *Positive Parenting*, which I co-authored with Dr. Ursula Schwartz, an excellent child psychologist. I also recommend *Make Me, Don't Break Me* (Moshe Gans, Mesorah Publications) and *How to Talk So That Kids Will Listen, and How to Listen So That Kids Will Talk* (Faber and Mazlish, Avon Books).

While techniques on how to relate to children are important, the greatest parental influence is *modeling*. Children may or may not do what you tell them to do, and are much more likely to emulate what they see you do.

Character is dependent on *middos* (fine character traits), and children are most apt to adopt the *middos* they see in their parents. If a child sees a parent lose control of his/her temper, all the lecturing, at home or in school, on the evils of rage may be of little avail. If the child sees significant bickering and discord between the parents with refusal to yield, they may have difficulty adapting to the needs and wants of others. If children observe selfishness in parents, they are likely to be selfish. If you want your children to be honest and truthful, show them that you value truth and honesty. Children do not distinguish "white lies" from lies of any other color. Cheating or deceiving that is somehow rationalized and justified is a lesson to children that dishonesty is acceptable.

Parents may not realize that they may be modeling unhealthy behavior for their children. For example, they may have a "Fuzzbuster" in the car to detect police radar so that they will not be caught violating the speed limit. They may not realize that the message they are sending to the children is, "It's okay to violate the law. Just make sure that you don't get caught."

Never underestimate young children. They are extremely perceptive. Precisely because their minds have not been cluttered with all the extraneous material that is in adult minds, they are exquisitely sensitive, much more than the most advanced lie detector. Do not try to put anything over on them. Be truthful and straightforward.

Children did not ask to be brought into this world. Doing so places an enormous responsibility upon parents.

Some mothers complain, "I don't know what to do for my child. He is not happy." We cannot *give* our children happiness, but we can give them the best shot at achieving happiness. Our prime concern in child rearing should be to give our children the best possible tools to be able to achieve a meaningful and happy life.

In my work of treating adolescents who have become drug abusers, parents regularly ask what they can do to prevent their children from using drugs. I tell them that many youngsters turn to drugs to seek *pleasure* as a substitute for the *happiness* they lack. In a home where each parent primarily seeks gratification of their own needs, children grow up with the feeling that such gratification is the goal in life. In a home where truly spiritual principles prevail and take priority over self-gratification, children are more apt to adopt a similar attitude, thereby decreasing the pleasure-seeking drive.

I wish you to have abundant *nachas* from your children. Remember, they are bound by the Torah to observe *kibud av v'eim.* The Torah repeatedly stresses the importance of *simchah* (e.g. *Deuteronomy* 28:47). By virtue of your bringing them into the world, you are bound by a moral responsibility to give them the best opportunity within your means to achieve true *simchah* in life.

Vignettes

*T*he marriage of Ezra and Adina was heralded as "the wedding of the year." The families had much in common, the couple was the image of compatibility, and there was no reason to postulate any differences that might lead to problems. What was not known, although perhaps it could have been known, was that Adina could not detach from her family. She was attached to her mother's apron strings, and she virtually worshiped her father. She said that she loved Ezra, but she took it for granted that Ezra would share in the admiration of her father and be totally self-effacing before him.

Although the halachah is that the wife should abide by the *minhagim* of the husband, this was unthinkable to Adina. Someone who did anything different than the way her father did was simply wrong. Although Ezra loved Adina, he could not see himself as being a mere appendage to her family. Whenever Ezra did anything even superficially divergent from the way her father did, Adina criticized and berated him. She eventually lost all respect for Ezra. Adina would not consider counseling because there was nothing negotiable. Suggesting that she respect Ezra's *minhagim* was tantamount to asking her to convert to another religion. Their child was born into a broken home.

The intensity of Adina's attachment to her family can be gathered from the fact that she refused to even consider seeing a marriage counselor. For what purpose? If Ezra would capitulate, there is no need for counseling. If he would not capitulate, there is nothing the counselor could say that would make any difference.

As much as parents wish to be admired by their children and may resist having the bond between them changed, they should prepare their children for the detachment that must occur with marriage. There can, of course, be continued closeness, but sons and daughters should be prepared for the healthy degree of separation that will permit a marriage to flourish.

*F*ischel and Ilsa's marriage got off to a rocky start. In the week of *sheva berachos*, he told her that all the decisions in their marriage would be made by him, because that's what the Torah says. Furthermore, he had a hero worship for his older brother, and would do nothing without consulting his brother. Ilsa felt that he was treating her as a non-person.

Ilsa suggested they go for marriage counseling. She felt that Fischel was not a bad person, just very immature at 21. She could get no help from his parents, because they thought of him as Mr. Perfect.

Fischel had great respect for his Rosh Yeshivah. Ilsa made an appointment with the Rosh Yeshivah and explained the problem. The Rosh Yeshivah had a talk with Fischel, and in a very gentle way pointed out to him that his attitude in marriage was not proper, and not at all *al pi Torah*. Fischel accepted the Rosh Yeshivah's recommendation for counseling, and the Rosh Yeshivah said that he wished to be apprised of their progress.

Several months of counseling was very effective in turning things around, and Fischel and Ilsa went on to have a very happy marriage.

*C*hezki and Chana had been married for six months, and everything in the marriage seemed to be going smoothly. Chezki was, therefore, taken aback when he came home one day and found Chana in tears.

"What happened, hon?" he said.

Chana tried to control her crying. "It's nothing," she said. "Never mind, it's really nothing."

"Honey," Chezki said, "you don't cry over nothing. Please tell me what's wrong."

"Bashi's wedding is two weeks away, and I don't have a dress for the wedding," Chana said tearfully.

"That's no reason to cry," Chezki said. "Two weeks is plenty of time to get a dress."

"My father would always ask my mother well in advance whether she had a dress for an event," Chana said. "You didn't even think of it. You're not considerate of my feelings."

Chezki said, "You're right, honey, but remember this. When you were old enough to observe your father asking your mother whether she had a dress, your parents must have been married for at least six years. When we're married longer, I'll know about such things, too. But we've been married for only six months. I never had a wife before. There are things I have to learn."

Chana wiped away her tears and laughed. "You're right. It was silly of me not to think of that."

Obviously, the dress was not the issue. Chana was hurt because she felt that Chezki was not being sensitive to her needs. She just needed to realize that it takes a while for spouses to learn about each other's needs. It is most important to keep this in mind during the first year.

*S*himon and Blumi had been married for three months when Shimon said, "Honey, I want to tell you something, but promise me you won't get angry with me."

Blumi said, "I promise, unless it's something really provoking. Right?"

"Okay," Shimon said. "You are probably unaware of it, but almost every other sentence, you end with saying 'Right?' So what's the big deal? It's just a bit annoying. Do you think you can try to stop that?"

Blumi said, "Why should that make me angry? I must have been doing that for years without being aware of it. Sure, I'll try."

A few days later, Blumi said to Shimon, "Honey, I want you to listen to something. I recorded this while we were having a conversation."

Blumi turned on the tape recorder. "Just listen to how you end every other sentence with 'Yeah.'" Shimon listened to how he said "yeah" at least as often as Blumi said "right." "Wow!" Shimon said, "I had no idea I was doing that."

Blumi smiled. "These are little habits of speech that we develop, but since it annoys you, I'll try to stop it. You'll remind me of it, right?"

Shimon and Blumi both broke out in laughter.

This incident may give the impression that Blumi was "getting even" with Shimon for finding fault with her. She did not intend her "cute" remark to embarrass him—she merely wanted to point out how commonplace her habit was.

In general it's commendable to hear what your spouse has to say and to try and correct an annoying habit without playing "tit for tat." Understanding that something you never noticed is grating on your spouse's nerves and trying to comply with his/her wishes is another way of expressing your commitment to your life together.

I received this query to my "advice" column, and here's my answer.

Query:

I've been married now for almost two years.

When my parents inquired about my husband for our *shidduch,* they were given excellent reports, and they are all true. He is a *talmid chacham* with good *middos.* The only thing they did not find out about him was his personality type, and this is something they probably could not find out because how can one measure personality?

Anyway, it turns out that as an *"ezer kenegdo"* I am about as *"kenegdo"* as it can get. I am a very emotional person. I easily get excited about things, and I react with elation when something good happens and I cry when something bad happens. I don't have mood swings so I am not manic-depressive. It's just that I react to things. I get things done satisfactorily. My house is clean, but I am not a perfectionist. Also, I could get along with a watch without a second hand.

My husband is just the opposite. He is very calculated, and rather cold emotionally. He takes things in stride, and is not moved in either direction by various happenings, good or bad. He is a perfectionist, and although he never criticizes me, I can tell he's not happy with my performance. And when it comes to time, seconds count. He is punctual to a fault. I think he'd be thrilled if I bought him a stop-watch for our anniversary.

It's not that we are unhappy. Not at all. I just wish there was some way we could minimize the differences in our personalities.

Response:

It is not necessary for a husband and wife to have similar personalities to have a happy marriage. If their personalities are too similar, it might actually be a rather boring relationship. Some *"kenegdo"* is desirable. You are saying that there is too striking a difference.

The important ingredients for a happy marriage are there, and that's what counts: a *talmid chacham* with good *middos.* The fact that he does not react the way you do does not mean that he is emotionally shallow. He may be very emotional but is not demonstrative. He may have a deep love for you, but is not the type to show it. There are families in which affection is not shown much, and that may be how he grew up. The fact that as a perfectionist he does not criticize you when things are not the way he would prefer indicates that he is considerate of your feelings, and that is important.

In every marriage, each spouse should make some adjustments to accommodate. In your case, a bit of effort to make small changes can decrease the gap between your personalities. You do things to your level of comfort, and it would take just a bit of effort to do a little extra, without becoming perfectionistic. For example, you know that he wants to leave for a wedding at 6:30, and you know it bothers him that you are not ready until 7. It does not take that much more effort to be ready earlier, even though it may go against your grain to do so. Similarly, although he may not have been emotionally demonstrative, he could make a bit of a change with some effort. He may have been raised in a non-demonstrative family, and showing emotion doesn't come naturally to him

You might say to your husband, "We really have a good thing going for us, but we can make it even better. I know you'd like me to do things more thoroughly and be more punctual, and I'm going to make the effort to do so, although it doesn't come naturally to me. I know that you are emotional, but showing your emotions doesn't come naturally to you. So let's each make the effort to go beyond what comes to us naturally." Because he is a considerate person, I'm sure he'll agree to try.

Don't expect dramatic changes overnight. Changing a habitual pattern takes time, but if you are both patient, gradual adjustments will occur.

Until One Hundred and Twenty

*T*he first year is indeed all important in laying the foundation for a happy marriage, but the effort to have a happy relationship does not end at the first anniversary. Although the Torah states that a husband is relieved of military duty and public service the first year of marriage, so that "he may gladden his wife" (*Deuteronomy* 24:5), it does not mean that the duty to make the wife happy is limited to the first year. In fact, such efforts must be increased *after* the first year, when the exemption of responsibilities expires.

As children arrive and as a husband becomes more involved in supporting his family, the time the couple can spend together is progressively limited. A myriad of distractions can take the husband and wife in two directions, with the possibility of diluting their intimacy. It is important to be on guard for such distractions, so that a distancing between the couple is avoided.

Too often, a husband and wife may spend quality time together only on vacations. At other times, their relationship may be only when they are free of other functions. In other words, daily activities may encroach on the time they have together, and these activities are given priority.

It may be necessary to *schedule* time together. We often set aside times for other things, times which are sacrosanct and during which we are not to be interrupted. It is advisable to have several hours a week designated as private time.

During the early part of marriage, mealtime can be a private time. Let the answering machine take the calls. Set aside time for a brief walk daily. On Shabbos, spend some time together reviewing the *parashah* or other Torah writings.

The marriage relationship is too often taken for granted. Just as a lawn requires upkeep to give it the necessary nutrients and to eliminate weeds, the same holds true for marriage.

All of the considerations recommended for the first year as enabling a good beginning should be continued throughout the marriage. Obviously, the nature of the relationship should mature with the advent of time, but mature does not mean "stale." Perhaps the pronouncing of the wedding *berachos* over a cup of wine may symbolize that just as wine improves with age, so should the marriage relationship strengthen and become more meaningful, with deeper love and consideration as the years progress.

My dear newlyweds:

May Hashem bless you with a happy marriage and much *nachas* together for one hundred and twenty years.

I am going to continue this book with advice for those people whose life circumstances resulted in a second marriage. There are many issues that require special attention.

But don't put this book away yet. Rather, go back to page one and reread it.

Ramchal, in his introduction to *Mesillas Yesharim* (*Path of the Just*) recommends rereading it many times. He says that precisely because he discusses things that are generally known, people tend to take them for granted and may not give them serious consideration. Therefore, rereading is necessary to keep these important guidelines in our minds.

Much the same can be said about what you have read. The guidelines for a truly happy marriage may appear so obvious that we assume we are already implementing them. My clinical experience tells me that this is often not true. We may need constant reminding about what makes a happy marriage.

May Hashem bless your marriage with *gilah, rinah, dizah vechedvah, ahavah, achvah, shalom, v'reius;* joy and gladness, mirth, glad song, pleasure, delight, love, brotherhood, peace and companionship.

Should you choose not to read the following section, skip to the Epilogue for a wrap-up. But perhaps it won't hurt if you do read on. There will be some discussions about marriages that failed and why they failed. This is an opportunity to learn from other people's experience so that you do not make the same mistakes they did. This gives you additional information to make your marriage long-lasting and happy.

A New Beginning

*E*verything that has been said in regard to newlyweds applies to a second marriage as well. Obviously, there are many other important considerations.

Many second marriages are happy and successful, and more could be if the couple would realize that there may be potential problems and prepare themselves to deal with them.

Even if this book were twice as long, it could not possibly address all the issues involved in a second marriage. There are many things that are not foreseeable, and a couple should have an understanding that unexpected things may occur and decide how they will go about dealing with them. Knee-jerk reactions must be avoided.

*K*alman and Shayna felt secure that they would have a smooth course. Kalman's three older children were married, and his 12-year-old son lived with his ex-wife. Shayna's older children were also married, and her 13-year-old daughter related well to Kalman. Shayna and Kalman both worked, and had sufficient income. Nothing to be concerned about, right?

Kalman's ex-wife then married a man who lived in Paris. She said that there was no way she could take her son to France. He had a learning disability and would be unable to pick up a new language. The psychologist said that the move for him would be traumatic. He had to stay with his father.

The boy had a behavior problem, and a conflict soon flared up between him and Shayna, and between him and Shayna's daughter. Kalman was caught in the middle. The boy was disrespectful to Shayna and aggressive toward her daughter. Kalman knew that he had to protect Shayna and her daughter, but he felt a loyalty toward his son and guilty for having left the marriage and putting the boy in an untenable situation. This was unanticipated, and in spite of Kalman and Shayna's best efforts, the difficulties progressed. By the time they sought professional guidance, the relationship between Kalman and Shayna had become strained.

Pre-marriage counseling is advisable in a first marriage, but is *absolutely essential* in a second marriage. True, the problem with the son could not have been dealt with in pre-marriage counseling because it was unanticipated. However, pre-marriage counseling would have prepared Kalman and Shayna to seek counseling at the earliest sign of a problem rather than waiting until it had impacted on their relationship.

Human beings are not robots. When we relate to another person with any degree of intimacy, that person has an impact on us. Whether a marriage ends by tragedy or divorce, the lost marriage is exactly that: a loss. And a loss must be adequately grieved if one is to put it behind oneself. Even if the first marriage was considered a failure, one must recognize its good aspects as well as its negative features.

If the first marriage was terminated due to the demise of one spouse, the widow or widower may face a variety of problems in remarriage. The children may understand that their father or mother should remarry, but nonetheless there are children who resent the parent's remarriage as if this were an affront to the memory of the deceased parent. The parents of the deceased spouse may feel awkward in visiting their grandchildren, whose new "mother" or "father" has replaced their child. These feelings may impact on the second relationship. The new spouse may feel that he or she cannot expect to be loved as much as the first spouse and therefore may not act or react in their normal fashion.

The time and effort necessary for adjustment in a second marriage are much greater than in a first marriage. The period of adjustment is at the very least *two years*, and maybe even longer. Yet, some people are so impatient that when problems arise, they decide that the marriage is a failure within the first few months. This is a mistake, and it is unfortunate that premature decisions are so often made.

The reasons for dissolving a first marriage are legion. Yet, although such reasons were undoubtedly present in the past, the incidence of divorce has skyrocketed in recent years. In the general population, the increase in the number of divorces in the U.S. was a mere 2 percent between 1950 and 1960. However, in the next ten years, the increase was 80 percent, and in the next decade there was another increase of 68 percent. At this point in time, marriages, which were once thought of as being forever, have no more than a 50-percent chance of survival.

Although the incidence among Jews may not be that high, there has been a significant increase in divorce among Jews. Inasmuch as 80 percent of men and women who divorce marry again, the number of "bi-nuclear" or blended families in the Jewish community has greatly increased. Although there are many potential problems in these families, many people are convinced that love, patience and understanding will enable them to overcome all difficulties. When they discover that this is not quite true, they may become disillusioned and may despair of the second marriage being successful.

There are many cases where a couple divorced because they "fell out of love." When the romance phase of the marriage was over, they became more aware of points of dissatisfaction which had been overlooked. As was noted in Part One of this book, when the basis for the relationship is primarily the desire of each partner for gratification of his/her own needs, frustration or inadequate gratification of these needs weakens the bond between them.

When a couple divorces because they feel that the marriage was not adequately gratifying, they are vulnerable to being attracted to a person who they feel can do a much better job of providing for their needs than the first spouse. This attraction may result in their overlooking what they later discover to be shortcomings in the partner. Indeed, their hindsight may even tell them that their "ex" had been a better mate, and their regret at leaving the family may engender guilt, which is certain to impact negatively on the second marriage.

Many second marriages are indeed happy and successful, but the likelihood of success depends not only on the willingness to make adjustments, but also very greatly on one's self-awareness. It is all too common to place the blame for failure of the first marriage on the spouse. It is axiomatic that we are much more aware of other people's shortcomings than our own.

Having written rather extensively about the pivotal importance of self-esteem in emotional health and the destructive effect of low self-esteem on relationships, I was pleased to find support for my position in *The Second Time Around* (Dr. Louis H. Janda and Ellen McCormack). The authors make these important statements: "You have to learn to live with yourself before you can live with anyone else" (p. 5). A person is not living with "oneself" if he/she has a distorted idea of that self. They cite the statement by Robert Burns, that we "must see ourselves as others see us" (p. 45). One's self-image may be radically different from how one appears to others. Yet, a person with a poor self-image may feel certain that other people see him as the inadequate and undesirable person he considers himself to be. And finally, "It takes more self-awareness than most of us are capable of to recognize when we, and not our partners, are responsible for our relationship problems" (p. 45).

Regardless of whether the first marriage was terminated by the death of a spouse or by divorce, one may think oneself to be better prepared for a second marriage. One may know that the initial passion is only a fleeting phase, one is more mature, and one may be financially more secure. One may, therefore, think that the adjustments to a second marriage may be easier than in the first, but one could not be more wrong.

A person who remarries following a divorce may say, "I realize what mistakes I made in my first marriage. These were too far gone to allow me to salvage my marriage by correcting them. I've learned my lesson, and by avoiding these mistakes, my second marriage can be successful." If only this held true more often! Psychologists speak of the "repetition compulsion," which means that a person may feel compelled to repeat a behavior even when he realizes that it is wrong.

Sometimes stories convey an idea more convincingly, so let me share with you a story that my father was fond of telling.

*I*n the days of horse-and-buggy, a traveler alighted from the train and asked a coachman to drive him to his destination. "But please," he said, "you must avoid that particular road, because there is a deep ditch in the road."

The driver said, "Just sit back and relax. I've been driving these roads for thirty-five years."

As they proceeded, the passenger said, "Look, I see where you're heading. Don't take that road. It has a deep ditch." Again the driver reassured him, "Just relax. I've been driving these roads for thirty-five years."

Sure enough, the driver took that particular road, and the passenger said, "Stop now! Just ahead of you is that deep ditch." Again the driver reassured him that he had been driving these roads for thirty-five years. But they soon fell into the deep ditch, and as the driver emerged from beneath the wagon, he said, "Strange thing! I've been driving these roads for thirty-five years, and whenever I come by here, this is what happens."

I think that by telling this story numerous times, my father wished to make me aware of the phenomenon of "repetition compulsion." We may know where the pit is, yet we may take the same path again and again.

There are invariably carry-overs from the first marriage. It is common that people who have been frightened by a trauma may develop a phobia for things that may have only a superficial resemblance to the traumatic event. Similarly, a woman whose first husband was alcoholic may become terrified if her new husband takes a drink. A man who was unable to tolerate the "nagging" of his first wife may react to something his second wife asks of him as if it were "nagging," even though she only mentioned it once.

A spouse who suffered from the first spouse's tyrannical control may react to something he/she is asked to do as if this were controlling behavior, although it may not at all be control.

While all the possible difficulties in a second marriage cannot be discussed, we can look at some of the more common problems. If you have read Part One of this book, you are familiar with these vital components of a successful marriage, but they are worth repeating.

- realistic expectations of marriage

- ability to identify and communicate feelings

- understanding the gender difference

- ability to resolve conflicts

- understanding true love

- a common spiritual goal in life

These were described in Part One, and apply equally to second marriages. Indeed, as important as they are in a first marriage, they assume even greater importance in a second marriage and demand attention by both spouses.

Motivation

*I*n Part One we noted that there may be some unrealistic expectations in marriage, and young men and young women who are motivated by unrealistic expectations are likely to be disappointed when these expectations are not fulfilled. This is equally true of second marriages, but there are additional factors that must be given consideration.

Emotions are very tricky. We may have strong feelings that we identify as love, but there may in fact be other emotions that have taken on the guise of love. The problem is that one can be deluded, and what one thinks to be love is actually the result of other feelings.

For example, the "rebound phenomenon" is well-known. In the case of a divorce which was not by mutual consent, one spouse may feel rejected. The insult of being rejected may be very distressing, and when one feels accepted by someone in a new relationship, this can be a very soothing balm for one's pain. This feeling of relief may be so comforting that it may make one think that he/she "loves" the "rescuer." In fact, however, this feeling is a reaction to the relationship that failed rather than genuine love.

Another feeling which is a reaction to the first marriage is when someone chooses a new partner out of spite; i.e., "I'll show him/her." Spite may sometimes result in the person marrying someone whom the "ex" did not like. This is hardly a healthy basis for a relationship.

A not uncommon motivation for re-marriage is "the children need a father/mother." If both partners recognize that this is the reason for their marriage, they may do their utmost to be the needed father/mother. The problem with this motivation is that it may go unrecognized, and one may deceive oneself that one feels true love rather than that one is marrying for the children's sake. If, as may happen, the children do not take well to the stepparent, and there really was no true love, the marriage is on shaky grounds.

I must repeat here what I wrote in *Ten Steps to Being Your Best*:

> It is undeniable that there is a component of the human being which is unique to man and is absent in animals. This component is often termed "soul" or "spirit." In medicine we are familiar with "deficiency diseases," which are the result of the absence of one of the body's essential nutrients. If the body lacks iron, there is the "iron deficiency syndrome," manifested by anemia and easy fatigability. If the body lacks vitamin C, there is the "vitamin C deficiency syndrome," with capillary fragility, bleeding gums and easy bruising. Physicians know the symptoms of deficiency diseases, can test for them, and can correct the condition by prescribing the missing nutrient.
>
> But we have posited that humans have a component in addition to the body, which is the spirit or the soul. Very much like the body, the soul, too, has essential nutrients, without which it can be symptomatic. The nutrients for the soul are the mitzvos and *middos* (character traits) which are essential for the spiritual well-being of a person. Absence of these nutrients results in a "spirituality deficiency syndrome," which is

manifested by a *pervasive discontent and unhappiness.* This discontent is not the same as clinical depression, and is not relieved by antidepressant medication. It is relieved only when the soul is provided with its specific essential nutrients.

Unfortunately, it does not occur to most people that their discontent is due to a spiritual deficiency. Rather, they attribute it to any of a variety of causes, and may seek relief by eliminating what they likely consider to be the cause. One person may blame his job or occupation and change these. Another person may try a "geographic cure" and relocate. Yet another person may fault the spouse and divorce. Inasmuch as none of these addresses the true cause, the discontent persists. The attitude of the "spirituality deficient person" is, "If there is anything wrong with me, it can be fixed by something outside of me," and one looks for a quick-fix, a magical cure. Turning to magical cures is a desperate attempt to fill a spiritual void with a material reality, and it is doomed to failure."

A person may divorce because he/she blames the spouse for he/her discontent. In such cases, the second marriage is not likely to eliminate the discontent. At the beginning of the marriage, the novelty of the new relationship and the expectation that the new spouse will provide what the first spouse could not may give temporary relief of the discontent. However, if the real cause for the discontent was lack of spirituality, the second marriage may be no more successful than the first.

I realize that I may sound like a broken record, because I constantly invoke the issues of self-concept and self-esteem in all emotional and psychological problems. However, I feel vindicated by an insightful statement made by Dr. Neil Clark Warren (*Finding the Love of Your Life, Pocket Books*): "A marriage can only be as healthy as the least healthy person in that partnership." I feel certain that lack of emotional well-being undermines a marriage. This is true of first marriages, but is even more important in second marriages. Whether the first marriage was terminated by divorce or death of a spouse, feelings of low self-esteem may exist, and raising one's self-esteem is extremely important.

If your first marriage was terminated by divorce, you may be so focused on all the shortcomings of your ex-spouse that you may pay little attention to your own shortcomings. You may bring these into the second marriage, which certainly does not bode well for its success. Therefore, it is important that you consult an objective person who can assist you in making a more accurate assessment of the failure of your first marriage. Even with all the faults you found in your ex-spouse, you may discover things about yourself that should be corrected.

In cultures where first marriages are arranged by *shidduchim*, the parents of each partner generally do their homework to find out whether the match is appropriate, and whether the two are likely to be compatible. The young man and the young woman do not meet until both sets of parents have approved. Although this method is not foolproof, it has allowed the couple to meet a few times, and if they feel the "chemistry" is right, they become engaged and may indeed have a good relationship (especially if they read Part One of this book).

This is generally not the case in second marriages, where one is on one's own to evaluate the compatibility of the partnership. More meetings are necessary to get to know the other person better, and as I have pointed out, counseling before committing to the relationship is extremely advisable.

A very legitimate motivation for a second marriage is that one does not wish to be alone. Indeed, this is the reason the Torah gives for marriage: "It is not good that a person be alone" (*Genesis* 2:18). However, we have all had the experience of being very hungry and eating something that was not good or us. This can happen with the craving for companionship. It may be so intense that one may seek to resolve it with an inappropriate choice. It is wise to seek the advice of a spiritual counselor and devoted friends as to the appropriateness of one's choice of a spouse.

It is understandable that people seek happiness, and people who have suffered a loss in life may look to a second marriage to make them happy. If the motivation for remarriage was the pursuit of personal growth rather than the pursuit of happiness, people would understand that "growing pains" are a fact of life, and could take difficulties in stride. This approach would have a constructive "side effect," providing the happiness they desire.

Carry-overs

*I*n every second marriage, there is inevitably some baggage brought along from the first marriage.

Whichever way you cut it, there is considerable discomfort in divorce. Even if a spouse feels that the other spouse was *entirely* at fault (which is unlikely), there may nevertheless be a feeling of guilt for the failure of the marriage. Whether or not this guilt is justified, it is there and may be a source of difficulty. But even if the first marriage was terminated by the death of a spouse, guilt feelings may occur.

Guilt is of two types. There is legitimate guilt for having done something wrong, and this guilt should be addressed by proper *teshuvah*, which consists of sincere regret and making amends to the offended person wherever possible. The Torah recognizes that human beings are fallible and may do wrong, and provides *teshuvah* to enable a person to divest himself/herself of the guilt. Once proper *teshuvah* has been done, the words of the prophet should be remembered: "I have erased your willful sins like a cloud and your errors like a mist—repent to Me, for I will have redeemed you" (*Isaiah* 44:22). Once a cloud or mist have been cleared, there is no longer any trace of them. The person who has done true *teshuvah* should feel redeemed and free of guilt.

The second type of guilt is more difficult to deal with. A person may feel guilt which has no basis in fact. A typical example is that of "magical thinking." For example, a person felt very angry at another person, and this second person dies. It is not unusual for someone to feel that his hostile wish caused the person's death. This kind of guilt is not relieved by *teshuvah* and requires therapy.

Even in the best of marriages, two people who have lived together for many years may have had moments of sharp disagreements which they patched up. Nevertheless, if one should die, the surviving spouse may feel guilty for having made unpleasant comments. Another example is that of a man who died of a heart attack, and the wife chastises herself for having allowed him to work so hard. She may feel that if she had made fewer demands on him, he would not have exerted himself so much. Even if there is no justification for this feeling, it may nevertheless bother her.

Whatever the type and source of the guilt, it can have detrimental effects on the second marriage. To avoid recurrence of guilt, either spouse may suppress any disagreement, yielding to the other on everything, but seething with anger at oneself for one's submissiveness, and at the other for making "unreasonable demands." The wife who faulted herself for her husband's heart attack may become overly-protective in the second marriage. She may exhaust her energies, and her husband may interpret her concern for him as "mothering" him.

The second spouse of a widowed person may have lingering doubts whether the partner has forgotten the first spouse or whether he/she is comparing him/her to the first spouse. Also, the widowed spouse may think it unjust that he/she is going to have an enjoyable life, while the first spouse was deprived of a longer life. One may think, "Would he/she have wanted me to remarry? Would he/she approve of the person I am marrying? Is this fair to his/her memory?"

*N*achum and Zelda had been married for only a few years when Zelda developed a malignancy. Several years after her death, Nachum remarried. During this time, he advanced professionally, and was able to provide his new wife with luxuries which he had not been able to give Zelda. His ambivalence toward living a more affluent lifestyle resulted in his being unable to fully enjoy it, and his second wife felt the impact of his guilt.

Unresolved grief or guilt feelings may infiltrate and erode a relationship. It is, therefore, advisable to consult someone before embarking on a second marriage to see whether there are unresolved feelings that should be addressed.

Dr. Parrott makes the observation that "The biggest challenge will be that you will soon discover that you've married two people: your new spouse and their former partner" (*Saving Your Second Marriage Before It Starts*, Zonderman Publishers p. 30). Two thousand years earlier, the Talmud stated that if each party to a marriage had been married previously, there are *four* people in this marriage (*Pesachim* 112b). The Talmud says this is equally true whether the first marriage was terminated by divorce or by death.

Halachah suggests that a widow who remarries should not observe her husband's *yahrzeit* nor visit the cemetery, and the same holds true for a widower (*Pischei Teshuvah Yoreh Deah* 403:2). However, it is not at all unseemly for him to call his children and remind them to observe their mother's *yahrzeit*. Birthdays and anniversaries are days that were characterized by emotions, and emotions are not subject to legislation. The attempt to make believe that there was no previous emotional relationship is doomed to failure. It is much better for both partners to realize that memories of the past cannot be eradicated, and to feel free to talk about them. They should let each other know what makes them uncomfortable.

If the first marriage was terminated by divorce, and especially if the divorce was the result of displeasure with the spouse, it might seem that there would not be lingering memories. That is not true. There were certainly pleasant moments on vacations or other occasions. If the new couple vacations in Hawaii where the spouse had vacationed in the first marriage, there will be memories.

If memories of the first spouse continue to linger, competent counseling should be sought.

No one enters a marriage thinking of the prospect of divorce. The statistics that more than half of second marriages end in divorce are ignored. Hope and optimism are wonderful feelings, but they should not stand in the way of reality. Second marriages can be happy and enduring, but this will require a commitment to make the marriage work, patience and the willingness to make personal adjustments. Let me reiterate, the period of adjustment in a second marriage is, at the very least, *two years,* and maybe even longer. The large number of second marriages that fail is due to impatience and unwillingness to make adjustments in the interest of preserving the marriage.

Earlier I mentioned that our attitude toward many things in life may have been influenced by the lack of tolerance and patience spawned by the marvels of technology. On the one hand, jet planes, microwave ovens, fax machines, instant foods and other time-saving devices have eroded our ability to wait. We may want instant results in everything, and when these are not forthcoming, we may give up. This is why we must be very cautious not to give up when the desired bliss of a second marriage does not occur immediately, and when there are problems that need to be resolved.

Second, as mentioned, our technology has given us a plethora of "disposables,"so that there are many things we replace rather than repair. Whether or not we see it this way, this attitude may have contributed to the dissolution of the first marriage. It is important that we make every feasible effort to overcome differences and difficulties in a second marriage, and not jump to the conclusion that it was a mistake when there are problems in adjustment.

Reactions can be affected by previous marriage experiences. Think of it this way. A person who develops a slight cough usually makes light of it. If, however, that person had a serious lung disease twenty years earlier which had begun with a cough, he may become alarmed over what is actually a rather innocent cough.

Similarly, if the ex-husband had a drinking problem, the wife may react with anxiety when she sees her husband take a *L'Chaim.* If her first husband was abusive, she may panic if her husband raises his voice. If the ex-wife was a spendthrift, the husband may become concerned over what he thinks was an unnecessary purchase. If the first wife neglected him by spending many hours with her friends, he may think that it is a repetition of the same when she spends even a reasonable time with friends. If either spouse was irritated by the ex-spouse's chronic tardiness, one may react with anger when the new spouse is late.

The best way to avoid improper reactions is to express one's reason for concern. For example, "Please understand that when I see you take a drink it conjures up painful memories for me. It will take some time for me to adjust." Or, "You had every right to spend time with your friends, but please understand why I reacted. This was a sore spot with me." Or, "I'm sorry that I reacted that way when you didn't call to tell me that you were delayed. I was reacting to a chronic and inconsiderate lateness problem in my first marriage. Let's keep in touch by cell phone and notify each other when we're delayed." By clarifying one's reasons for reacting, misunderstandings can be avoided. It may take months or even a few years to get over a conditioned fear that resulted from unpleasant experiences in the first marriage.

In Part One I underscored the pivotal role of trust in marriage, stating that trust is the cement that binds the couple. It is especially important to remember this in a second marriage. Quite often, the reason for dissolution of the first marriage was a breach of trust. This may result in a carry-over of suspicion and lack of trust into the second marriage. This is why issues that were factors in the problems of the first marriage should be dealt with in individual therapy before embarking on a second marriage.

Is This Person Right for You?

*T*his question is germane in both first and second marriages. As was noted, many first marriages are arranged by *shidduch*, where the parents' involvement in finding an appropriate companion may result in avoidance of unsuitable partners, whose incompatibility might be overlooked when passion prevails. In such cases, the couple may not meet each other too often. In second marriages, or in cultures where the couple dates more frequently during the courtship, the couple themselves are more likely to determine their compatibility.

The popular wisdom, "Trust your feelings," may not be the best advice. As we have repeatedly noted, emotions can obscure and distort reality. What, then, should one be looking for?

*O*ne of the wisest suggestions was voiced by a woman whose first marriage ended unhappily. "Having had a bad experience in my marriage, I decided that when I met a man, I would look for the things I *don't* like about him, and then say to myself, would I be able to tolerate these annoyances for the long term? I had no thoughts like I did with my first husband that I could change him and that he would come around for me.

"I ended up marrying a man whose frequent mention of his first wife when we dated drove me up a wall. We did not like the same foods. He likes classical music and I like jazz. It doesn't bother him to be 15 minutes late for a date, whereas I'm punctual.

"I gave it much thought. The positives about him outweighed the negatives. I was frank with him about the things that annoyed me. The things that irritated me during our courtship still irritate me, but they are tolerable. I had no compunction that I would change him. He didn't deceive me and I didn't deceive myself.

"We are in the sixth year of our marriage, and we're getting along just fine."

This woman's mature thinking about what she did or did not like about a man enabled her to avoid the self-deception that may occur in romance.

As a fledgling psychiatric student, I learned something from a patient, a young woman who was hospitalized because she acted-out at home. In our interviews, she would go into a tirade about her mother, who was just a terrible person.

On the second weekend, she asked for a pass to visit home. "Why do you want to go home?" I asked.

"I want to see my mother," she said.

"I thought you said that your mother is a terrible person," I said.

"She is a very terrible person," she said.

"I don't understand," I said, "Then why do you want to go home?"

The young woman said, "What is it that you don't understand? She's my mother, so I love her. But there's nothing about that woman that you can like."

It took an emotionally disturbed young woman to enlighten me that "love" and "like" are not synonymous.

Perhaps it is more important to marry someone you *like* rather than someone you *love*. Liking someone means that the person has admirable traits that you can respect and appreciate. Liking may be free of the passion of "love," which can render you oblivious of things that may be intolerable over the long haul.

Here are some helpful guidelines.

Do you like the way he/she reacts to stressful situations, or how he/she deals with other people who are upset or angry? Do you make excuses for how he/she reacted to a situation? ("She was just very upset," or "He's been under a lot of stress.") If the answer to the first question is "yes" and to the second question "no," that's a favorable prognosticator. If it's the reverse, watch out!

Are you anxious to introduce him/her to your family and friends? If you're hesitant because you think, "He/she is really a good person, but you have to get to know him/her. They might not appreciate him/her the way I do." "Yes" to the former is a positive; "yes" to the latter is a negative.

Do you share many ideas and positions; e.g., about religion, politics, social issues, art, literature, music, philosophy? You don't have to be identical twins by any means, but neither does the colloquial proverb "opposites attract" mean that polar opposites can have a good relationship.

You may know a couple who are perfectly happy although they are as different as day and night. He is an introvert, she is an extrovert. He hardly says a word, she is loquacious. These may be the differences that are obvious, but their similarities may not be as apparent. They may share many common interests, and are more alike in some of the things that really matter.

Go back to Part One of this book and review the more common gender differences. Are you okay with that? Also reread the chapter on "control." If you see controlling tendencies, beware! Let me remind you again, do not plan on changing him/her.

Financial Issues

*T*he role of money in a second marriage cannot be downplayed. It is, of course, important that both spouses make full disclosure of their financial status. Discovering indebtedness or undisclosed commitments after the marriage raises reality problems as well as resulting in lack of trust and a feeling of having been deceived. It is even worse if the undisclosed commitments are alimony and child support.

Even if the husband is forthright and disclosed his financial commitments to his first family before the marriage, and even if the new wife agreed to the terms, there may still be trouble. She may say, "Yes, you told me that you had obligations, but I never imagined they would impact us so heavily. Why, you're making a good salary and we're living at the poverty level."

A very unpleasant situation may result when the family finances are strained due to the husband's paying alimony and child support to the first wife, and the new wife's income helps defray these. She may feel and may say, "I have to work to take care of her!" Imagine what she feels like if the first wife lives in greater comfort, while they have to count their pennies. If the first wife is vindictive, she may make unrealistic demands, backed up by a threat of dragging the husband into court.

Money problems may occur in first marriages and may cause unpleasantness, but this does not compare to what may occur in a second marriage.

*S*ender and Naomi together earned enough to be able to live comfortably. However, the alimony and support payments to Sheila drained their finances. Although Sender was current in his payments, he received a letter from Sheila that their son needed dental work which was not covered by insurance, and would he please *promptly* remit $900 to avoid going through a court action. Sender was irate, and Naomi broke down in tears. "We'll never be able to get ahead," she said, adding very angrily, "My car spends half the time in the repair shop while Sheila runs around in her BMW." When Sender's children visit, dressed in designer clothes, Naomi is very bitter that she has to shop at bargain stores for her children.

Sender had considered his financial status before remarrying. He had received a promotion and a salary increase, but his new position had necessitated moving from Philadelphia to Memphis. Whereas paying for his children's transportation was not an issue when he lived in Philadelphia, it now meant two airplane tickets twice a month. He had not taken that into account. When the children come, Sender tries to give them a good time and takes them out to eat, but he and Naomi cannot afford to eat out. Naomi had hoped they would have a child together, but that would mean quitting her job, which would significantly reduce their income. It is not unheard of for a person to be driven to the point of bankruptcy as a result of an ex-wife's demands and legal maneuvering. It is not easy for a couple to keep their composure under such circumstances.

Absolute honesty about their financial conditions may forestall some problems. A man should not be offended if the woman he wishes to marry asks to see his income-tax returns for the three previous years. If a child applies for a student loan, such information is requested. Although marriage is certainly a very different situation than applying for a student loan, and one may feel that a wife should have more trust in one's integrity than a loan officer, it is nevertheless not an unrealistic request.

Again, although there may be unforeseen financial problems which cannot be dealt with in pre-marriage counseling, the latter can provide preparation on what the couple would do in the event that unanticipated financial problems did occur.

Although there should be much optimism about the success of the second marriage, it is wise to avoid "painting oneself into a corner." For example, if one moves into the new spouse's house, one need not sell one's house immediately. Rather, rent it out. Why? Because if a problem does develop in the marriage and one feels "stuck" in the marriage because one has no place to go, this adds stress that can hinder resolution of the problem. Keeping ownership of the previous house is not an expectation that the marriage is likely to fail, anymore than having home insurance is an expectation that the house will be burned down. If possible, irreversible decisions should be avoided until there is stability in the marriage. This enables both spouses to adjust more comfortably.

In addition, the prenuptial agreement should clearly and irrevocably state what belongs to the surviving spouse in the event one of them passes on. This is extremely important, so that the deceased's children will not have conflicts as to what is theirs and what belongs to the spouse.

Adjusting: Acceptance and/or Coping

*T*here are not too many certainties in life, but one of them is that life is full of challenges: little challenges and big challenges. When confronted with a challenge, there are essentially only two options: *coping or escaping.* Each person develops his or her own pattern of dealing with challenges. How we deal with challenges is important even in a first marriage. However, since the couple is generally young, they are usually both confronted with the challenges, and they may develop ways of dealing with them. In a second marriage, both partners are generally older and have weathered many challenges, each having developed his or her own way of dealing with them. Their methods may be very different, which can give rise to conflict.

My work with alcoholics has provided me with abundant examples of how people deal with challenges. It is particularly enlightening to note the methodolgy of people who have recovered from alcohol addiction and its many complications. Many of these people have recovered with the help of the Alcoholics Anonymous fellowship, and I have been privileged to learn from them.

Each meeting of Alcoholics Anonymous opens with the non-denominational prayer, "G-d, give us the serenity to accept those things we cannot change, the courage to change those things we can, and the wisdom to know the difference." This brief statement may indeed be the secret of optimal adjustment to life's situations. *Do not try to change the unchangeable.* That is a waste of time and effort, resulting only in disappointment and exhaustion. On the other hand, do not resign yourself to situations which *can* be improved. There is no reason to suffer needlessly. Apply your skills to remedy remediable problems. And be wise enough to know which is which.

Some people attack every challenge with great gusto, while others shy away from anything that appears to be a difficult task. If a couple differs significantly in their approach to challenges, it may give rise to problems. The wife may accuse the husband of being rash and foolhardy, undertaking things beyond his ability, and the husband may accuse the wife of avoiding anything that requires some courage, or vice versa. It certainly makes for a much smoother relationship if there is a general agreement on how to deal with challenges.

Inasmuch as both partners to a second marriage have undoubtedly experienced a variety of challenges, it would be helpful if they would do a simple exercise. Here is what I suggest you do:

Each partner should make a list of several of the difficult situations they encountered. A sheet something like this may help them clarify their reaction patterns.

1. Challenge

_____

_____

Ways in which I coped (positive/negative)

_____

_____

Ways in which I escaped (positive/negative)

_____

_____

2. Challenge

_____

_____

Ways in which I coped (positive/negative)

_____

_____

Ways in which I escaped (positive/negative)

_____

_____

The more challenges that can be listed, the better. Do not hesitate to elaborate on how you dealt with the challenge. There are many ways of coping and many ways of avoiding a challenge.

After completing the assignment, *compare notes.* Ask each other, "How would you have handled this situation?" and if your reactions differ, try to figure out why you each respond differently. This simple exercise can help you get a better understanding of each other and enable you to more or less predict what the other's response is likely to be when confronted with a challenge. Most importantly, this exercise may help you to learn more effective ways of dealing with the tough spots in life. We sometimes develop a pattern of reacting which becomes habitual, and we react to situations without considering all options.

Here is another helpful comparison.

Both of you should list a few things that send you into a rotten mood, like getting stuck in traffic or being stood up for an appointment. These are unpleasant for everyone, but people's responses may vary. (I was once stuck in traffic for two hours. After seething a bit, I remembered that I had two tapes of Luciano Pavarotti that I had just bought. Inasmuch as I wasn't going anywhere anyway, I decided to enjoy a fabulous concert.) Write down how you usually feel in such situations and how you react. Compare notes. You may not only develop better reactions to such stresses, but you may also get to know more about each other. Then realize that the two of you can team up to cope with the negatives that may occur in marriage.

If you and your spouse differ in your approach to things, this is where the *ezer kenegdo* is very constructive. It gives you the opportunity of learning from each other.

In *Ten Steps to Being Your Best*, I pointed out that whether a person chooses to cope with or to escape a challenge depends on two things: the assessment of the magnitude of the challenge, and the assessment of one's capabilities.

In my office, there is a poster of birds in graceful flight. The caption reads, "They fly because they think they can." Very often, people escape rather than cope because they underestimate themselves. If a person can be helped to a more realistic awareness of his personality strengths, his self-confidence and self-esteem is appreciably increased. By comparing and discussing how they dealt with challenges, a husband and wife can not only arrive at a more uniform way of managing things, but also gain in self-awareness and self-esteem.

A Blended Family

*A*ll that can be done about this topic is to highlight a few of the many possible issues. There are so many variables that it is impossible to cover them all. This is why pre-marriage counseling is so important. Issues that were never considered may arise, and unless one is prepared to deal with them, one may respond with a knee-jerk reaction, which is rarely constructive.

There have been many second marriages with blended families where everything worked out okay, but there have also been many situations where there were profuse heartaches. Planning the operation of the blended family may help avert much distress.

I wish that there was some term other than "stepfather" or "stepmother." We have been so suffused with stories about wicked stepmothers that the prefix "step" has an unpleasant connotation.

But like it or not, the blended family has a stepfather, stepmother, stepchildren, and stepsiblings, to which there may be additions of half-brother and half-sister. There are also step-grandparents.

There is a difference whether all the children are married and living independently or whether there are some from either or both families still at home. In the latter case, a number of issues need to be dealt with.

In all likelihood, you are not going to give up both homes and move into a new residence. You will probably be living in one of your two homes. If you will be living in your husband's residence, there will be many of the first wife's things around. Not necessarily personal stuff, but furniture, kitchenware, dishes, etc. Her children are likely to associate these items with her. When you, as the new wife, use these items, it may strike an emotional chord with the children. Furthermore, you may not feel comfortable in using "her things." You may feel that not only do the children have emotional associations with these things, but perhaps your husband does, too. These items may appear as some kind of attachment to the first wife.

If you live in the wife's residence, the same is true. You may be lounging in their father's favorite chair. You sit at the head of the table where their father sat. You may be reading his books. It may not be practical to totally overhaul a home and replace everything in it.

In either case, the children who grew up in that house may see the new children as invaders who are encroaching on their property and using what was once totally theirs. Both spouses must be prepared to deal with their own feelings and prepare the children for this challenge.

You may say, "Your children are going to be to me just like my children." This is simply not true. Not only do you have a biological tie to your children, but you have also invested much energy in them during their growth. You cannot possibly feel the same to your new spouse's children as to your own, and it is a mistake to say that you do. If, in fact, you do, then that would be abnormal.

There may have been a time when budgetary considerations did not allow you to give all your children what they all wanted. There may have been other considerations as to why one received something that the others did not. When your 14-year-old daughter was given a trip to some place, there may have been many reasons why you could not do the same for your 12-year-old daughter. You did your best to explain it to her, and she had to make peace with it. It's entirely different if there is a valid reason for your not giving *your spouse's* 12-year-old daughter what you give *your* 14-year-old daughter. As a stepparent, all the explanation in the world may not eliminate the suspicion of favoritism and discrimination.

Children require discipline, which, understandably they resent. However, they generally accept discipline from their parents, albeit grudgingly. Even with both biological parents, children are very adept at playing one parent against the other. This is exponentially increased when the discipline is by a stepparent. The biological parent and siblings may gang-up against the stepfamily in a holy war.

Especially at the beginning of a second marriage, discipline should come primarily from the biological parent. You and your spouse may write the rules for the house, but the biological parent should enforce them. Later in the marriage, your new spouse can become more involved in discipline.

*E*li was a very easygoing person who could not assert himself to discipline his children in his first marriage. He tolerated their misbehavior. He felt that his second wife, Zelda, having been a schoolteacher, would be able to control them. However, whenever Zelda did try to discipline them, they went to their father, who yielded to their wishes. Zelda was never able to enforce the consequences of their misbehavior. Since the biological parent did not assert himself as disciplinarian, the mayhem that resulted nearly ruined the marriage.

As mentioned in Part One, there are differing schools of thought on what discipline method is preferable, and each school claims best results. The important thing is that both parents should abide by the same method and be supportive of each other.

Inasmuch as Part One of this book is a guideline for the first year of marriage of young newlyweds, the problem of abusive behavior toward children does not occur. It does occur that a mentally deranged parent can be abusive even to a newborn, but I am not addressing that kind of parent. In a second marriage, however, there may be children who require firm discipline, and efforts to exercise discipline may deteriorate into abuse.

What constitutes physical abuse? It is generally held that anything that leaves black and blue marks on the body. However, even without visible traces, excessive force of any kind is abusive and generally counterproductive.

Rabbi Moshe Leib of Sassov saw a coachman whipping his horse. He said to him, "If you knew how to communicate with your horse, you would not need to whip him. Why should the horse have to suffer because of your ignorance?"

We may not all have the skills of communicating with animals, but we should be able to communicate with people, even children. Use of force is an admission that one is lacking the knowledge of how to communicate. Why should children suffer because of an adult's ineptness at communicating?

Verbal and emotional abuse do not leave black and blue marks on the body, but can inflict serious damage on one's psyche, damage which, unlike black and blue marks, does not fade with time. Belittling a child's performance, calling him insulting names, or showing preference for other children can cause a child to think of himself as inadequate or inherently bad. This may seriously impair the child's ability to develop his innate abilities and to have self-respect.

What happens when the children require discipline and the biological parent is away? The same thing that happens when parents put a babysitter in charge, saying "We expect you to listen to Martha when Daddy and Mommy are away." Similarly, the biological parent should make it clear that when he/she is away, the step-parent is the authority. When the biological parent returns, he/she can reinforce the step-parent's authority by supporting him/her in the children's presence.

If the first marriage was terminated with hard feelings, it may not be easy to behave civilly toward an ex-spouse, but it is extremely important that you do so. The reality is that your ex-spouse is still a vital part of your children's lives. They have to feel free to love the other biological parent. They may wish to talk about him/her. If your present spouse is uncomfortable with this, try to help him/her accept this. At the very least, you should be open to your children's talking about the other biological parent.

Children of a divorce have enough on their hands without having to choose one parent over the other. They should never be put into such a position. If the two households have two sets of rules, adjustment is possible if the children are not made to show preference. Any harsh feelings one may have toward an ex-spouse should never be conveyed to the children. One does not gain loyalty of children by turning them against a biological parent, even if that parent was abusive to them.

A very difficult situation occurs when one parent is Torah observant and the other parent is not. The Torah observant parent may be very upset that when in contact with the ex-spouse, the children are encouraged to eat nonkosher food or violate the Shabbos. Reasonable parents, knowing that putting children in such conflict can be harmful to them, will consider the children's well being. Regrettably, not all parents are reasonable. When such conflicts occur, the help of a rabbi with competence in marital problems should be enlisted.

If you are a stepparent, remember that biological ties are strong and unique. Don't expect to replace a biological parent. This is especially true when that parent is no longer alive. Let the step-children set the pace for the relationship, how much affection they want from you and how much authority they are willing to give you. Many stepparents do have loving and warm relationships with their stepchildren, but you can't assume this will be so, and you may feel awkward in not being able to play a full parental role. If you will try to act as though you were a biological parent, the stepchild is likely to say, "I don't have to listen to you. You're not my real father/mother." And remember, don't allow your spouse to make you the disciplinarian of your stepchildren.

Allow your stepchildren to have time alone with their father/mother. They may see you as a competitor for the biological parent's attention. Don't make this into a battleground. Back off, and allow them adequate "alone time" with the biological parent.

Sometimes, a stepparent may so wish to demonstrate devotion to the stepchildren that he/she devotes more time and energy to them than to the spouse, giving their needs priority. This is not good for the marriage relationship, and although it is his/her biological children that are getting the attention, the spouse feels left out. If you form a solid relationship as a couple, you become better parents together. This eliminates the parents' feelings of being caught in the middle between the children and the new spouse.

A stepparent's good intentions may backfire.

*B*aruch had a 17-year-old son who had just gotten his driver's license and wanted to borrow Naomi's car. Baruch thought that by letting him do so, it would help forge a bond between his son and the stepmother. Well, Naomi did not see it at all that way, and was very upset at the boy's using her car. It is not wise to make assumptions. Asking Naomi would have been appropriate. Perhaps if she allowed him to use the car, it might have helped the relationship, but Baruch's generosity with her property did nothing for the relationship.

If you have different traditions, respect the traditions of the other family. Sometimes a rather minor practice can have great significance.

*S*halom had two sons and Chava had a son. It was Shalom's practice that on Friday night, he made *Kiddush* and *hamotzi* for the family. Chava's son was accustomed to making his own *Kiddush* and to have two small *challah* rolls for his own *hamotzi*. Shalom's insistence that Chava's son be covered by his *Kiddush* like his own two sons did not sit well with the boy or with Chava. Shalom was insensitive.

What about *birchas habanim* (blessing the children Friday night). Does the stepfather bless only his biological children or the stepchildren as well. Will they feel awkward, ("You're not my real father") or will they feel left out if not blessed? This decision should be made by the stepchildren. You may say (well in advance of Friday night), "A *berachah* is valuable from everyone. If you wish, I'll be happy to give you the *berachah*, but if you prefer otherwise, I will respect your wish."

A word of caution about communication with your ex-spouse. If he/she is a reasonable person, there should not be any major problem. But if he/she makes unreasonable demands, you have to set matters straight. Problems that should be handled by an attorney should be referred there. If it appears that he/she calls primarily to annoy, get caller-ID and make it clear that while you are available to deal with realistic issues, you will not respond to what you see as annoyance or harassment.

Above all, *don't put your new spouse in the middle.* You may be tempted to say, "Here, you talk to him/her. He/she is driving me crazy." Also, if you are talking to your ex-spouse, don't allow your new spouse to coach you on what to say. You may say to your ex-spouse, "I have to think that over and I'll get back to you," and this will give you the opportunity to discuss it with your new spouse. If you are the new spouse and your spouse receives a call from his/her ex-spouse, it is wise to leave the room and not be present during the conversation.

It may be helpful to hold family meetings, acknowledging that there may be issues, and that it is best to discuss them so that an optimum adjustment can be made for everyone. It is best to schedule a set time for the meetings, so that everyone can prepare for what they wish to discuss. Decisions that are made where everyone has had a chance to voice an opinion can be very bonding, even though not everyone's opinion is enacted. (However, don't hold these meetings during meal time.)

There are also extended family issues to consider. When a spouse celebrates a child's Bar Mitzvah, must one invite all the relatives of the other spouse? Zisha's extended family was quite small, so all his relatives could be invited, but Naavah's extended family was very large, and this could be a huge financial burden. And what if there happen to be interfamily squabbles? Or, Betzalel's parents were both living, but Tirzah's parents were gone. On Chanukah, Betzalel's parents gave their grandchildren Chanukah gifts, whereas Tirzah's children had no grandparents. Any number of extended family problems may occur.

Researchers say that it takes *at least three years* for a blended family to begin acting like a family. It is normal for there to be difficulties. Things can be worked out, but both partners must be very patient and be able to exercise restraint.

In many communities there are seminars and support groups for stepparenting. Take advantage of them. There is no substitute for experience, even someone else's experience.

Gender Differences

*I*n Part One I mentioned that there were gender differences that should be acknowledged by both spouses in order to avoid mis-understandings. It is even more important to be aware of these in a second marriage.

Contrary to the erroneous opinion that marriage, by making a person more mature and more responsible, will improve his charac-ter defects, the fact is that very often, whatever one has been as a single, one becomes *even more so* after marriage.

In a first marriage, the children may forge a bond between spouses. In many second marriages, the couple does not have children together, and when each brings their own children into the marriage, they are more likely to be a divisive rather than a unifying factor.

Many character defects are a result of unmet or unrealistic needs, and the particular behavior may be the way one defends one's fragile ego. The termination of a marriage by divorce is invariably a blow to one's ego, rendering a person more sensitive. Hence, one's pre-existing psychological defenses may be accentuated. Gender differences that might have been brushed aside in a first marriage may take on greater significance.

Our psychological system is divided into two major parts: the cognitive and the affective, or, another way of putting it, the *thinking* and the *feeling*. The Talmud states that women are generally more emotionally sensitive than men. Women may be every bit as bright as men, but whereas men tend to act and react according to how they *think*, women tend to act and react more by how they *feel*. The culture values the "macho" in men, which means that men are encouraged to suppress their feelings. By virtue of this, they may not be aware that the wife is more vulnerable to emotions than they are.

Here is one scenario. A wife emerges from an unhappy marriage with much frustration that her emotional needs had not been fulfilled. She is hoping that her new husband will be more giving emotionally and more considerate. However, having suffered rejection in his first marriage, he is very defensive. He is hesitant to allow himself to feel for fear of being hurt again. Neither of the two have dealt with their feelings and have not discussed these issues. Somehow, each assumes that the other partner will understand. Well, too often the other partner does *not* understand.

If there is passion in the marriage, it may cover up these differences. However, inasmuch as the intense passion eventually fades, the wife may see her husband as distancing himself from her. He seems to be operating much more with his head than with his heart. Her needs for emotional nourishment are frustrated, and she may become disillusioned. This is not what she had hoped for. She may become angry and try to retaliate, or to protect herself from emotional hurt, she may go numb.

The husband may sense the wife's dissatisfaction, and because he is a "thinker" and a "problem solver" rather than a "feeler," he may try to make his wife happy by buying her things. While she certainly appreciates this, it does not satisfy her needs for warmth and companionship, and her frustration continues. The husband now becomes upset, not understanding why she is unhappy. "Nothing I do can make her happy." He does not understand that the shortcoming is not in what he *does*, but rather in what he *is*.

He misinterprets her reaction to him as rejection, which resurrects the pain in his first marriage. To protect himself from rejection, he withdraws, which further aggravates his wife. It is easy to see why this marriage may be headed for real trouble.

While marriage counseling may save the marriage, the axiom "An ounce of prevention is worth a pound of cure" applies. *Prior* to considering remarriage, each spouse would do well to have individual therapy to gain greater insight into oneself and to divest oneself of the baggage from the first marriage. Once the couple is seriously considering marriage, they should have pre-marriage counseling to understand their expectations from one another and to better understand gender differences, as well as discuss some issues that may arise in combining two families.

With proper preparation, a second marriage can be a very happy one.

The Prenuptial Agreement

*I*n first marriages, there is generally no prenuptial agreement, although having one could avoid many problems. The last thing a young couple would consider is that their marriage may fail. However, given the unprecedented incidence of divorce, there is ample justification for a prenuptial agreement even in a first marriage.

In second marriages, it is extremely important to have a prenuptial agreement. In addition to various considerations for the spouses, both partners usually have children and should protect the property rights of their children. Failure to do so can result in much painful confusion and litigation.

The *tenaim* (articles of engagement) is a kind of prenuptial agreement. Someone is honored with reading the *tenaim*, a dish is broken to the cheers of mazal tov, and everyone is happy. This is definitely *not* the case with a legal prenuptial agreement. This document is drawn up by two lawyers, each representing one of the partners.

Lawyers are invariably involved in adversary proceedings. Each lawyer is on the defensive, trying to get the best deal for his client and to outsmart the opposition. This is the mind-set of lawyers, and they approach the prenuptial agreement as though they were representing adversaries, rather than a couple who wish to share their lives. Their attitude may wear off onto the couple, who are then driven into adversarial positions. In addition, the legal terminology of the prenuptial agreement is enough to put anyone on the defensive.

I have seen situations where the quibbling of the lawyers impacted on the couple, resulting in the cancellation of the marriage and the breakup of a relationship.

Keep this in mind when doing a prenuptial agreement. Let the lawyers fight it out between themselves, because that is what they are accustomed to doing. Have them give you the agreement they propose, then you and your betrothed sit down together to review it. Make sure to tell each other that you are not out to "get" the other partner, and that you are doing this only to avoid future misunderstandings. Make whatever changes you both agree upon. If you have differences, consult a marriage counselor who will not look at you as adversaries. *After* you have come to an agreement, tell the lawyers to write it up. Do not allow the lawyers to tell you what you need. Both of you come to an agreement and tell *them* what you want.

Once the prenuptial is signed, put it away in the safe-deposit box. Hopefully, you should not need to look at it again.

Midlife Changes

*I*nasmuch as most second marriages occur a bit later in life, they may coincide with the phase that is often referred to as "midlife." There is also a popular term—"midlife crisis." It is important to know something about midlife, because if the problems common to this phase are not recognized, one may attribute them to the marriage and mistakenly view the marriage as a failure. Dr. William Nolen, author of *Crisis Time*, claims that every man, sometime between age 30 and 60, and especially between 45 and 55, goes through a midlife crisis. Sometimes he hides it from others, and at other times he is not even aware of it himself. Dr. Nolen says that more marriages are crippled or destroyed by midlife crisis than by any other single entity!

The equivalent of midlife crisis in women is the menopause or "change-of-life," which is now recognized as being due primarily to hormonal changes. There may be emotional symptoms ranging from mild to very severe. A variety of regimens are available to relieve the symptoms of menopause. While the physiologic changes in men are not so pronounced, it is believed that there are some biochemical changes in men that can result in depressive symptoms.

Not too long ago, it was thought that menopause was purely a psychosomatic condition, due to the woman's awareness that she was losing her youth. Although the physiologic causes are now widely recognized, the psychological effects of feeling that one has "turned the corner" cannot be dismissed, and these are as common in men as in women.

In their younger years, many people are ambitious and have high aspirations. When these dreams are not realized by the mid-40s, a person may abandon these ambitions. "If I have not made it until now, I am never going to make it anymore," and a feeling of resignation sets in. A person may feel very vigorous at 48, and may be shocked to discover that he cannot compete for jobs with younger people. Industry favors youth, and being refused at 48 because one is "too old" can be depressing. Technology continues to come with gadgetry that is more rapid and more efficient. Younger people take to these like a duck to water, while these sophisticated apparatuses may be incomprehensible to an older generation. We live in a culture that worships youth.

Midlife is also a phase when one's children are establishing families. When the children are small, there are a myriad of problems, and parents may look forward to the time when the children will be grown and independent. This may certainly come to pass. However, there is a wise Yiddish saying, *"Kleine kinder=kleine tzoros; grosze kinder=grosze tzoros"* (little children=little problems; big children=big problems). The midlife years are hardly worry free.

Somewhere around this time, we become aware that we cannot remember names. We may be embarrassed to meet someone socially whose name we knew well, and now we cannot recall it. We may remember perfectly something we learned thirty years ago, but not remember what we learned yesterday.

People in midlife quip that the telephone company is using smaller print in the telephone directory, that people who used to speak clearly have started to whisper and mumble, and that the incline in the walk from home to shul has been made steeper. Because of these changes, they may need reading glasses and hearing aids, and must leave a bit earlier for shul. Joints that we never even thought of begin to make their presence known. Although we have many years of life ahead of us, we may sense that our prime is well behind us.

In previous times, there was at least a redeeming factor in growing older. Seniority was revered. This took a strong hit in the 60s, when anyone over 35 was considered to be obsolete. Today, we can look forward to some economic concessions as we grow older, but not to the esteem in which age was once held.

The physical and social factors combine to produce any number of symptoms. There can be insomnia, especially awakening in the early a.m. and not being able to fall back asleep. There may be excessive worry over things that do not warrant deep concern. There may be irritability. There may be a decrease in libido and loss of interest in things. To relieve these distressing feelings, a man may have recourse to alcohol, tranquilizers, or sleeping pills, on which he may become dependent. Although these may temporarily ease his symptoms, their effect is to depress the brain, which may actually aggravate the condition.

It is not unusual for men in midlife to become fed up with their job. Lawyers find that their cases are no longer stimulating, and doctors find their practice boring. Hungry for something to give color and flavor to life, men who are widowed or divorced may feel that marriage will provide the missing spice. A new relationship may indeed provide some excitement, but when the novelty of the relationship wears off, the midlife symptoms recur.

Dr. Nolen says that the most helpful thing in midlife crisis is *someone with whom the individual can speak about his problems— a sympathetic listener.* Who else is best suited to provide this relief other than his wife? Dr. Nolen continues, "It's odd that once two people get married, they soon run out of things to say to one another ... After ten years of marriage, monosyllables constitute the bulk of most husband-wife considerations. This is because they think they know each other so well that conversation isn't necessary ... The man and woman who will sit down together at least three times a week for half an hour and unburden their souls to each other will avoid many of the problems that others encounter, particularly in midlife."

It is very tempting to write more extensively about the midlife crisis, but that is not the thrust of this book. But whether it is universal, as Dr. Nolen contends, or just quite common, both men and women can contribute much to their happiness and preserve their marriage by familiarizing themselves with the midlife phenomenon.

Many people think that they are immune to midlife crisis, perhaps because they think of it as being a character weakness. A while back I was one of several lecturers in a series aimed at people age 40-55, on how to prepare for retirement. The lectures encompassed physical health, finances, and social and psychological issues. It was well advertised, but very few people enrolled. It was clear that people deny the possibility that they may have problems as they get older. A similar denial operates in regard to mid-life crisis. However, failure to recognize and understand it may result in very unwise decisions.

Having listed all the negatives that may begin at midlife, let me say that there is no reason for surrendering Our self-esteem should depend on how we feel about ourselves, and not on how industry looks at us. Young people may indeed be more adept at electronics, but there is no substitute for the wisdom of experience.

I recall a baseball game in 1951, when Andy Pafko, a 44-year-old major league veteran, was playing right field. The batter hit what appeared to be a sure home-run, but Pafko leaped up and grabbed the ball just as it was about to clear the fence. The sportscaster went crazy with astonishment. "He caught the ball! Imagine, a man of 44 (which is very old in baseball) could jump up to make that catch!" The announcer's assistant said, "You've got it all wrong. A younger person might be able to jump better, but only someone with Pafko's experience could know the precise timing to make the jump."

Do not give up your ambitions! I suggest reading the book, *Late Bloomers,* by Brendan Gill (Artisan Publications). These are accounts of people who established their careers at a time when others were retiring. The book you are now holding is my forty-sixth. Thirty-eight of these were written after I was 55, and twenty-five were written after 65. Sure, I have to scrounge for words that once came to me automatically, but so what? I could not have written these books at 35 nor even at 45. Perhaps I had easier access to words at an earlier age, but I didn't know what to do with them.

Nevertheless, we may grieve the loss of our youth, and if, in the early years in a second marriage, we do feel less energetic or even depressed, we may wrongly attribute it to the marriage. As was noted in the previous chapters, there are a host of problems that may present in a second marriage, and if we are subject to any of the midlife changes, we may implicate the problems in the marriage as being the cause of our lassitude or mood.

Precisely because there are some depressing factors in midlife, we need each other *more* rather than less, and a couple should focus on ways in which to be more supportive of each other.

A Mutual Mirror

*A*lthough this book is intended to be a guide for the first year of marriage, and there are a number of books that elaborate on fulfillment in marriage, I do wish to add something to the concept of "wholeness." As was said earlier, the sages refer to man as whole only when he is married.

The term *ezer kenegdo* is generally thought to describe the function of the wife. A bit of thought will reveal that when one person stands *keneged* (vis-a-vis) another person, the latter also stands *keneged* the former. The *kenegdo* is thus a mutual rather than a unidirectional concept.

The Baal Shem Tov stated that "the world is a mirror." Inasmuch as a person is often oblivious to his/her own shortcomings, the Baal Shem Tov said, but he has no difficulty in seeing those of other people, G-d arranges it so that he should observe *his* character defect in another person. He should know, therefore, that the defects he sees in others are those that are true of himself.

*T*he chassidic masters took this very seriously. R' Menachem Mendel of Lubavitch (Tzemach Tzedek) was receiving his chassidim for individual sessions. Abruptly, he told his aide that he cannot see anyone because he needs a period of solitude. After several hours, he again began to receive his followers.

The Tzemach Tzedek explained, "When I see and hear the shortcomings in others, I try to find them within myself. When I do, I can take proper steps to correct these defects. In the last person, I saw a defect which I could not find the slightest trace of in myself, regardless of how diligently I searched. This meant that I must be in denial of it. I therefore had to pray and meditate and do a thorough soul-searching to overcome my denial, until I was able to find a trace of that defect in myself."

We can now understand why "It is not good for man to be alone." A person without anyone to relate to is at the mercy of his denial, and cannot become aware of his shortcomings. G-d, therefore, gave Adam someone who could serve as a mirror, *kenegdo*, and by the same token, he would serve as a mirror for her.

It was not only because Adam was the only human being on earth that he needed a mate to be *kenegdo*. "It is not good for man to be alone" is as true for us today as it was for Adam, even though there are now several billion people in the world. No one has the capacity of being a mirror in the same way a husband and wife can be for each other. It is unfortunate that this unique opportunity is too often neglected.

Many, if not most, of our character defects have their origin in our biological composition. A human being is a composite creature, comprised of a physical body and a spirit. The body is, for all intents and purposes, an animal body, with all the drives and urges of an animal. What makes man unique is those features that are absent in an animal, such as the ability to think about a goal and purpose in life, the ability to improve oneself, and the ability to make moral and ethical decisions in defiance of bodily drives. In contrast to animals, which are uninhibited and give free reign to their biologic drives, it is expected of a human being to be master over his biologic drives rather than a slave to them. However, it is a mistake to deny and disown one's biological composition.

The Midrash states that when Moses ascended to heaven to receive the Torah, the angels protested, arguing that mortals do not deserve the Torah and that it should be given to them. G-d told Moses to rebut the angels' argument. Moses said, "The Torah says, 'Do not covet your neighbor's wife.' Does that apply to you?" Moses continued pointing out that all the prohibitions in the Torah are meaningless to angels, who do not have the capacity to do these things. The Torah was given to man precisely because man *does* have the urge to do these things. It follows that the 365 Scriptural prohibitions indicate that there are 365 acts that a person may be tempted to do. If any of these were alien to man, there would be no need for the prohibition, just as there is no need for angels to have these acts forbidden to them.

Both man and woman are subject to all the drives of animals: anger, greed, lust. power, and a variety of self-centered drives. There are indeed some gender differences, but there are far more similarities than differences.

Every person develops ways in which to deal with or exert mastery over his/her animalistic drives. Some ways are more efficient, others less. Some ways may give rise to defense mechanisms that may be counterproductive. *Many character problems and difficulties in relationships can be traced to inadequate management of our human-animalistic nature.*

Although there are indeed biological gender differences and certainly sociologic gender differences, there are nevertheless many things that are common to both genders. For example, it is conceivable that there is a qualitative and/or quantitative difference in anger between men and women, and there are certainly sociologic differences that influence how men and women deal with anger. Nevertheless, anger per se is a biologic emotion that is present in both men and women.

Anger is an emotion that may present difficulty in management. The various phases of anger were discussed earlier, and we noted that a person may be completely unaware of having repressed anger. Repressed emotions may sometimes find circuitous ways of expression, but a person may be oblivious of how this occurs in himself. However, one who is unaware of anger-related features in himself may have no difficulty in detecting them in others.

Let us consider the Baal Shem Tov's teaching that the defects one sees in others are a reflection of one's own. A wife realizes that her husband has difficulty with anger management of which he is unaware. According to the Baal Shem Tov, she should conclude that she, too, must have a problem with anger management of which she may be unaware. Having been alerted to it, she is now in a position to do some introspective searching. She may read up about anger management and may discuss it with someone. Her husband's serving as a mirror thus gives her an opportunity for self-improvement that she might not get otherwise. The same is true if the husband detects a problem of anger management on the part of his wife. Thus, the *kenegdo* relationship, if properly understood and utilized, may allow for significant personality development in both. This holds true for all other character traits.

Inasmuch as the husband and wife are in an intimate relationship, the mirror phenomenon between them provides a much greater opportunity for self-awareness and character refinement than the mirroring of other people.

Self-improvement is predicated on a person's sincere desire to improve himself/herself and to invest the requisite energy to achieve this. It also requires the willingness to admit that one has shortcomings and to welcome the opportunity to discover them.

"He who loves reproof loves knowledge" (*Proverbs* 12:1).

Unwillingness to admit that one has character traits that need improving makes improvement impossible.

"Do you see a person who is wise in his own eyes?

For a fool there is greater hope than for him" (ibid. 26:12).

"Listen to counsel and accept reproof,

that you may be wise in the end" (ibid. 19:20).

As was noted, man's assignment is to develop himself spiritually, fulfilling the Divine wish of "Let us make man," to become the being that G-d intended. To the degree that a person does not correct his/her character defects, to that degree a person is not the "whole" unique being that G-d wishes one to be. The unique opportunity of mirroring provided in marriage enables the couple to achieve fulfillment of the Divine wish and to be truly whole.

Epilogue

*T*he Talmud states that (including the first two of the Ten Commandments which we heard directly from G-d), Moses gave us 613 mitzvos. King David condensed these into eleven principles, the prophet Isaiah further condensed them into six principles, the prophet Michah into three principles, and the prophet Habakkuk into a single principle (*Makkos* 24a). Clearly, no one detracted an iota from the 613 mitzvos. Rather, they sought ways in which one might more easily have a grasp of the entire Torah.

While all of the suggestions for a wholesome adjustment in the first year of marriage are important, I believe it is helpful to have a few basic principles which underlie all of them.

1. Husband and wife should respect one another. The principle, "The dignity of your fellow should be as dear to you as your own" (*Ethics of the Fathers* 2:13) applies even more to a spouse

than to others. No two people are of totally like mind, and some differences of opinion are inevitable. One need not agree with the other's point of view, but one should respect the right to have a dissenting opinion.

2. Not all disagreements must be promptly resolved. Open communication will eventually lead to a satisfactory resolution. Sometimes the best compromise is no compromise.

3. The focus should not be "what is best for me," but "what is best for us," and ultimately, *shehakol bara lichvodo,* "what is most conducive to the glory of G-d."

4. The couple should function as a unit. Your spouse is your best friend. Even when a spouse is *kenegdo,* one can be an *ezer.*

5. Stresses and challenges are opportunities for growth, not for retreat.

6. "May it be Your will that we see the merits of others, not their faults" (prayer of R' Elimelech of Lizhensk). If you are upset by something your spouse did, before reacting think of the many good things he/she has done.

7. Although marriage is a partnership, it does not always operate on a 50/50 basis. There are times when there may be far more give than take.

8. You've made your choice. Be convinced that it's the right choice and if perchance it isn't—make it work nonetheless.

9. Don't let problems fester—like a wound that is treated immediately, prompt attention will avert the need for major surgery.

10. Never do anything to undermine your spouse's trust in you. Trust that has been broken is nearly impossible to repair.

11. Make your home a place which will be inviting for the *Shechinah* (Divine Presence).

In the Torah community, much is learned about behavior by observing how Torah personalities act. We also have a rich literature about *tzaddikim,* especially those of the last few generations. One aspect of their lives is essentially unknown: how husbands and wives related in marriage. Relatively few people have or had access to the family lives of our *gedolim,* hence we could not utilize them as models for ourselves.

Some of the anecdotes that have been recorded reveal the devotion and dedication of spouses to one another. The theme of *shehakol bara lichvodo,* that G-d created everything for His glory, was central to their marriages.

In our own generation, there was a great Torah personality, R' Shlomo Zalman Auerbach. As great as he was in Torah scholarship, he was even greater in *middos*. Stories abound of his selflessness and unparalleled sensitivity and consideration for every man, woman and child.

When R' Shlomo Zalman's wife passed away after sixty+ years of marriage, R' Shlomo Zalman said, "It is the practice to ask forgiveness from the departed person for any offensive act that may have occurred. We lived all our years together according to the teachings of Torah, so there is nothing for which I must ask forgiveness."

This would be difficult to accept from anyone of lesser integrity than R' Shlomo Zalman, but we can rest assured that he was speaking the truth. Just think of it! Living in an intimate relationship with a person for over sixty years, and knowing that one had never acted in an unkind or inconsiderate way.

R' Shlomo Zalman was a great human being, but a human being nevertheless. Perhaps we cannot aspire to his vast Torah scholarship, but it is within everyone's means to behave in a manner that will give him no cause for regret.

Living according to Torah means much more than keeping a kosher home and observing Shabbos. These practices alone would not have justified R' Shlomo Zalman's statement. Living according to Torah means acting according to the *middos* prescribed by Torah. These can be found in the works of *mussar*. This is why I advocated that young couples institute the practice of studying *mussar* together, right from the start.

Gilah, rinah, dizah, chedvah, ahavah, achvah, shalom, reius—all these are within your grasp, but they are not deposited at your doorstep. The seeds must be planted and the field nourished. You can then reap the sweet fruits of a devoted relationship.